SQL Basics

Learn SQL the easy way

Fabian Gaussling

Contents

Preface

More than 40 years ago SQL was invented. SQL, that's the acronym for Structured Query Language and the concepts behind it are more relevant than ever. Nowadays a lot of data is generated and collected in all areas. Therefor it is important to handle those data correctly. For that SQL is still necessary. The concept of relational databases exists for several decades and one could not imagine life without it.

Nearly every application saves data in a database. Also a lot of hardware components like sensors, engines, etc. generate data. Based on this data totally new use cases for reporting occurred, like improvement of productivity, quality control, etc. Because of that SQL is getting more interesting for people from IT distant areas: engineers, medical staff, etc.

This book should be an introduction for everyone who is interested in SQL. The book starts with a chapter on theoretical concepts and basic terms followed by an overview on the course's data model. Chapter three deals with the creation and alteration of database objects (creating, changing and dropping tables, columns, constraints, etc.) as well as with the manipulation of data (insert, update, delete).

Chapter four to six are about basic query techniques (selecting columns, doing calculations, filtering data), joining multiple tables (inner and outer joins) and grouping & aggregating data. This is the foundation of every SQL query and when you've accomplished chapter 6 you are able to get most of your problems solved with the help of SQL.

The seventh chapter is on sub queries, a more advanced technique, which is needed for complex calculations when one single query isn't enough. Mostly that are questions that you could also solve with multiple standalone queries but in order to reduce manual work you can combine these standalone queries to a big query with many sub-queries. Chapter eight is dealing with set operations like union, intersection and exception.

The last chapter is a collection of multiple smaller topics like granting/revoking rights, smaller useful functions and an introduction to analytical functions.

Before you get started you should set up a suitable working environment for the exercises. For that you can download a guide on my homepage: http://gaussling.com/information/book_ressources_en You find information where to find the database software (Oracle, MySQL, Postgres, SQL Server) and how to install and configure the training database.

Now you can start directly into the world of databases and SQL.

Have fun reading this book!

Fabian Gaussling

1   Introduction to database systems

What is a database?

Almost everyone is familiar with Excel and has used it at least once in their lifetime. In Excel, you have worksheets consisting of many cells where you can enter different values (numbers, text, dates, etc.). These cells are organized in columns and rows.

For instance, if you wanted to manage addresses in Excel, you would probably enter the different data in different columns, e.g.:
- First name
- Surname
- Street
- ZIP code
- City

You could arrange the address data in rows, and the whole thing would have the following format:

First name	Surname	Street	ZIP code	City
Hugo	Schmidt	Sylter Weg 15	24145	Kiel
Bert	Meier	Schanzenstraße 1	20357	Hamburg
Egon	Müller	Exerzierplatz 3	24103	Kiel
Ivonne	Müller	Oldendorfer Weg 22	25524	Itzehoe

This constitutes an address table. We also have tables in databases, the so-called **database tables**. Every table consists of several **columns**, each containing different data. The rows are called datasets in database terminology. A **dataset** contains all columns that belong together. In our example, a dataset would consist all the columns of an address. Database tables contain different forms of data depending on the application.

In practice, you usually need more than one table (just like in Excel). You could have one table for customers, one for sold products, and another for the billings. The three tables contain very different data, but all three tables could be important for the order management of a pizza delivery service. When you combine several tables, we speak of a **database**. Different databases for diverse applications are managed in a **database management system (DBMS)**. Common examples include Oracle, Microsoft SQL Server, IBM DB2, etc.

One uses the so-called query language for easy access of the data in the tables. The query language enables you to tell the database the datasets that you need. Assuming you wanted to view Hugo's address from our previous example, you can use the **Structured Query Language (SQL)**. A simple example would look like this:

```
SELECT *
FROM TBL_ADDRESSES
WHERE Surname='Schmidt'
```

This would return all columns of the dataset that contain the surname 'Schmidt'. Such a language is particularly advantageous if you have tables containing millions of datasets or if you want to view

5

specific data from multiple tables at the same time (will be described in detail later). With that, we have successfully used our very first SQL in this course. Many more will follow. ;)

In addition to SQL as a query language, we also have the **Data Definition Language (DDL)** and **Data Manipulation Language (DML)**. The DDL is used to define the structure of a database, i.e. tables and their structures. Furthermore, a database also has numerous other objects (e.g., views, indices, etc.), which will only be touched on marginally in this course. The DML is used to fill, edit, or delete data in tables.

Relationships between tables

Most databases contain diverse tables in order to structure the data in an organized manner and avoid redundancies (see chapter on normalization).

The different tables are hereby **related** to each other. For example, if you have one table containing information about your customers and another for the orders, you would only need to add the customer numbers in the orders table and not the entire information about the customer. Having this customer number in both tables creates a relationship between these two tables. All the information about a customer (e.g., address, phone no., etc.) is only saved and managed once in the customers table instead of saving it multiple times in the database. For example, you can use SQL to determine how many orders have been placed by customers from a specific region by simply linking the customers table (containing the customers' place of residence) and the orders table. If a customer changes his/her address, you only need to update the table at a single point.

We use **ER models** (ER = entity relationship) to illustrate the relationship between tables via their columns. Below is an example of such a model:

Figure 1: A simple ER model

The relationships or links between tables are established via so-called keys. Here, a distinction is made between primary and foreign keys. **Primary keys** uniquely identify a dataset in a table. In the case of the customers table, this would be the 'customer no.'. This is marked with a "P" in the ER model to highlight the primary key. A **foreign key** is a reference to the primary key of another table (marked with "F" in the ER model), i.e. which dataset in the other table is linked to that of the current table. In the above example: Which customer dataset (primary key) is linked to which order (via the foreign key). Relationships are therefore always defined by linking a foreign key to a primary key.

There are different types of relationships in different tables:
1. 1:1 – relation
2. 1:n – relation

6

3. N:m – relation
4. Recursive relations

In the ***1:1 relation***, you only have one dataset in the foreign table for every dataset in the primary table and vice versa. As for the ***1:n relation***, you have 1 to n datasets in the primary table for every dataset in the foreign table. And for every dataset in the primary table, you only have 1 dataset in the foreign table. This is the most common case in practice. In our example, we have a 1:n relationship between customers and orders. Every customer can appear several times in the orders table. However, there only exists one customer for every order. ***N:m relationships*** mean that for every dataset in one table, you have n datasets in the other table. In relational databases, such a situation can only be modeled using an intermediate table.

Most DBMS allow you to ensure that the ***referential integrity*** is upheld. This means that every foreign key must always have a corresponding dataset in the referenced table. In such a case, it would not be possible to delete this dataset from the foreign table as long as it is referenced by another dataset. You can only delete it after you delete all the other datasets first. The same also applies in reverse. You must first create this dataset in the foreign table before referencing it from another table.

For you to always ensure this referential integrity, you must set up the so-called ***foreign key constraints***. This simply means defining the foreign-key relationships between two tables at a database level. We also have the so-called ***check constraints***. These are used to ensure that only certain values can be entered in specific columns such as if the column is only meant for the salutations 'Mr., Mrs., & Ms.'.

Normal forms

The following properties must always be ensured for easy and correct data evaluation:
- non-redundancy
- unique
- consistency

To make sure these properties are upheld, there are certain rules that must be adhered to in data models. These rules are referred to as ***normal forms***. There are five normal forms, each of which can be used to avoid specific redundancies that can arise in the data model. The first three normal forms are usually the most relevant and are described in detail using the contact information table below:

TBL_CUSTOMER	
CUSTOMER_NO	NUMBER
NAME	VARCHAR2 (20 CHAR)
ADRESS	VARCHAR2 (20 CHAR)
SEX	VARCHAR2 (1 CHAR)
TITLE	VARCHAR2 (10)
PHONE_NUMBERS	VARCHAR2 (100)

Figure 2: Example of customer data – starting point

A table in the ***1st normal form*** cannot have repetition groups and each of its attributes must be atomic (i.e. cannot be subdivided into other attributes).

Applied to our example, this means that we cannot have "Address" as an attribute since the address can be subdivided into street, ZIP code, and city (atomicity). If a contact can have several phone numbers, these should not be saved in the "Phone no." field (repetition group). We also cannot have fields "Phone_number 1" ... "Phone_number X" (repetition group). Instead, we could add an attribute called PHONE_NUMBER as part of the key (from a combination of the CUSTOMER_NUMBER and PHONE_NUMBER).

```
                  TBL_CUSTOMER
P * CUSTOMER_NO    NUMBER
    FIRSTNAME      VARCHAR2 (20 CHAR)
    LASTNAME       VARCHAR2 (20 CHAR)
    STREET         VARCHAR2 (20 CHAR)
    ZIP_CODE       VARCHAR2 (5 CHAR)
    CITY           VARCHAR2 (25 CHAR)
    SEX            VARCHAR2 (1 CHAR)
    TITLE          VARCHAR2 (10)
P * PHONE_NO       VARCHAR2 (100)
⊶ TBL_CUSTOMER_PK (CUSTOMER_NO, PHONE_NO)
```

Figure 3: Example of customer data – 1st normal form

The 1st NF basically makes sure that the data can be evaluated. If you were to save the entire address in a single attribute, it would be difficult, e.g., to sort and filter the data based on the place of residence.

The **2nd normal form** stipulates that given the table is in the 1st NF, every non-key field is dependent on the entire key and not just a part of the key. This ensures that a table only contains relational data. It also helps avoid inconsistencies since the attributes can only occur once.

In our example, this means that NAME, STREET, CITY, GENDER, and SALUTATION depend only on the CUSTOMER_NUMBER but not the TELEPHONE_NUMBER. If a contact was to have several phone numbers, the contact information would be redundant in the table thus consuming too much space (no longer a big problem today) and can also lead to inconsistencies. You would now create an extra table for phone numbers.

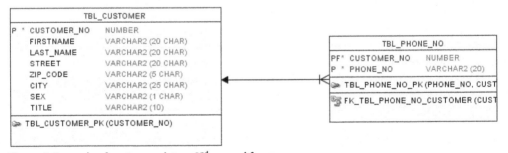

Figure 4: Example of customer data – 2nd normal form

To comply with the **3rd normal form**, a table must already be in the 2nd NF and non-key fields must be independent of other non-key fields. The 3rd NF prevents further redundancies.

In our example, this would mean that fields 'City' and 'Salutation' would be outside the attribute since the city is dependent on the ZIP code and the salutation dependent on the gender. This additionally helps avoid redundancies that would lead to inconsistencies.

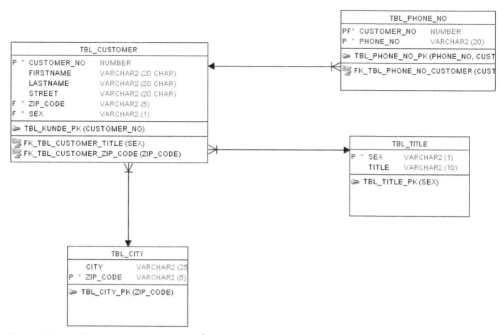

Figure 5: Example of customer data – 3rd normal form

The normalization increases the number of tables in a data model. Thus, queries can take longer since the tables must be linked to each other. In case the response times become too long, you can also *denormalize* the data models. This is usually common in data warehouse applications that have tables in the so-called star schema.

Database transactions

When adding or changing data in tables, it must be ensured that the data remain consistent. Here, one usually talks of the *ACID* paradigm:
- *A*tomicity
- *C*onsistency
- *I*solation
- *D*urability

The paradigm dictates that data changes must be *atomic*, meaning that a set of operations is either performed completely or not at all. In addition, it must also be ascertained that after the changes, the dataset remains *consistent* (as long as it was consistent before). The changes should be *isolated* so that different operations do not to interfere with each other (e.g., simultaneous deletion and reading of a dataset). The edited data must be saved *permanently*.

For all this to be upheld, we have the so-called *transactions* in modern DBMS. A transaction is more like a bracket with which one or more DML (insert, update, delete) instructions are handled as a block. The results are only saved after the individual instructions have been executed. After a transaction, the results can either be saved permanently using **COMMIT** or rolled back using **ROLLBACK**. The changes are only visible after a successful COMMIT.

Exercise

1. Modify the following data structure to obtain the 3rd NF. The data are hereby arranged in columns:

Country	ISO code	State	City	Branch	Employee	Contact data
Germany	GER	Hamburg	Hamburg	Spitaler Straße	Mr. Schmidt Mrs. Müller Mr. Meyer ...	Tel: 040-1234 Fax.: 040-1235 Email: Hamburg@enterprise.com
Denmark	DEN	n/a	Copenhagen	...	Mrs. Sörensen ...	...
...						

2 Introdcution of the training database

This chapter is based on the theoretical principles of databases covered in the 1ˢᵗ chapter and introduces the test database used in this course. It should also serve as a rough illustration of how database models are usually structured to meet actual departmental requirements.

Technical framework conditions

Schmidt Imbiss Group would like to save records of its <u>customers</u> and <u>orders</u> in a central database for practical data evaluation. Currently, the company has 4 <u>branches</u> in *Hamburg, Kiel, Lübeck, and Flensburg*. They sell a number of <u>products</u>, which can be categorized in <u>product groups</u>. This fact should also be depicted to maintain a clear overview if the number of products increase in future. Currently, every product has a price.

Customers can either pick up their orders directly at the store or have the products delivered to them. For this purpose, Schmidt Imbiss Group currently has *5 drivers, 2 cooks, and 3 sellers* tasked with the order intake and processing. The <u>employees</u> receive a *monthly base salary* as well as a *commission* based on the respective service. For drivers, the commission is based on the number of deliveries whereas for the sellers, it is based on the respective sales. At the moment, cooks only receive a fixed salary.

In addition, it should also be possible to evaluate the following attributes for the customers:

- *ZIP code and city*
- *Gender*
- *Date of birth*

A customer can place *more than one order*. Each of these *orders is processed by one seller*.

Deriving a logical model

Here, we can derive a simple logic model. We can first identify the key substantives (<u>underlined and highlighted in blue</u>). These include the candidates for subject-specific objects, e.g., customers, orders, etc. They have various attributes (customer no., first name, surname, order date, etc.) and are related to each other. Below is an illustration of only the substantive objects described above:

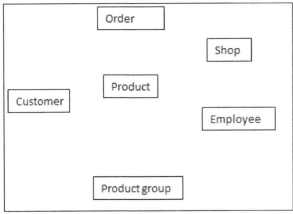

Figure 6: Logical model – 1ˢᵗ step

In the text with the technical description, additional interesting facts are written in italics and highlighted in red-brown. These can be verbs, but what should we do with them? They are properties of certain objects e.g., there seems to be chefs, sellers, and drivers. These are all employees but all have different tasks. You could now introduce individual objects for each employee type or an attribute type for the employee object describing this characteristic more precisely.

In practice, you will often be faced with the question whether to model certain aspects as a separate object or just as properties of an object. Here, it is important to ask yourself whether multiple attributes can be bundled under one new object. The golden mean is often the best option, i.e. not creating too many separate objects, and congesting everything under one object (keyword: normalization).

Now, if we were to add our known relationships in the logical model, we get the following model:

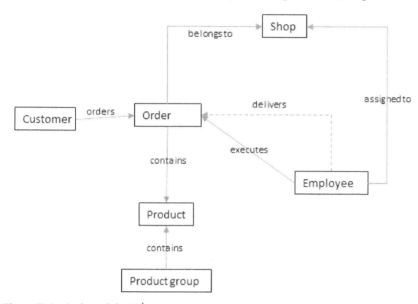

Figure 7: Logical model – 2nd step

The model is slowly taking after an ER model. We can now add cardinalities to the arrows between the objects and attributes. You will notice that this raises many questions. These must be clarified with the department and the model adapted accordingly.

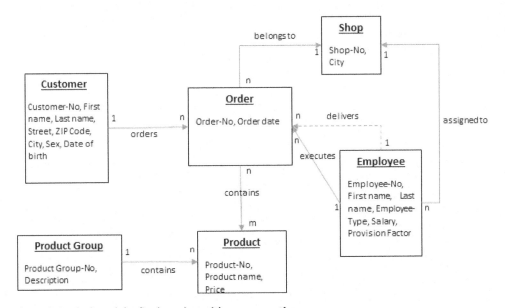

Figure 8: Logical model – final version with open questions

As you can see, we've added attributes to the objects. Some attributes will automatically come to mind e.g., the need for a customer to have a customer no., first name, surname, and delivery address. Other attributes were named explicitly in the technical description.

The same applies to the relationships and cardinalities. The fact that a customer can place several orders and that a product group can contain different products was mentioned explicitly. The same with the fact that an order processed by a specific employee is also assigned to the employee. I have added the second relationship between employee and order to specify the driver who delivered the order. Since this is a can-relationship, a dashed line is used.

Nothing was mentioned about the relation between product and order. Inquiries with the department revealed that every order can include multiple products and every product can also be ordered several times. Every product can also be assigned to several orders. This thus results in an n:m relationship between order and product, with the relation having one attribute, i.e. the number.

Deriving a relational database model

The next step would be to create a relational database model from the logical model. Here, a lot of information can be adopted. The n:m relation must be resolved via an intermediate table (TBL_ORDER_POS) since n:m relations cannot be modelled directly in relational databases.

The rest of the relations and cardinalities result in the foreign key relationships in the relational database model:

- A customer can place multiple orders. Every order is attributable to exactly one customer.
- An order has multiple items. Every item is attributable to exactly one order.
- Every item has exactly one product. Every product can appear in multiple items.
- Every product group contains multiple products. Every product appears in exactly one product group.

- Every order is processed by exactly one employee. An employee processes multiple orders.
- Each order can be delivered by one driver. A driver can deliver multiple orders.
- Every employee is assigned to exactly one branch. Every branch has multiple employees.
- Every order is assigned to exactly one branch. Every branch has multiple orders.

The final database model is shown on the next page.

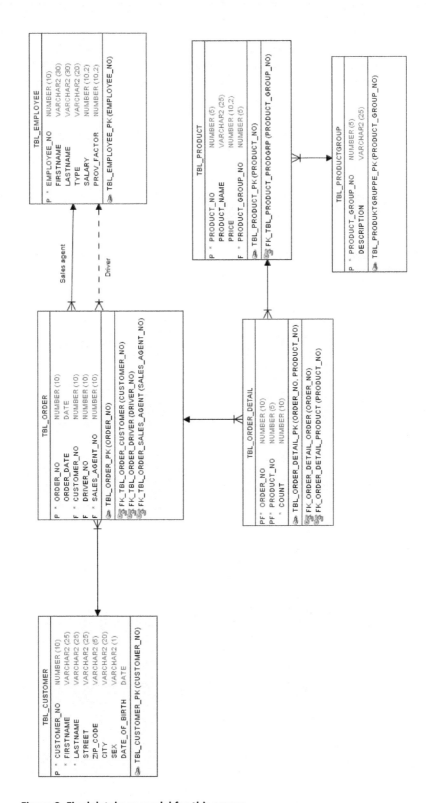

Figure 9: Final database model for this course

3 Creating simple queries

Select columns (SELECT)

In this chapter, we will create our first simple queries. We will only query data from a single table and gradually get to learn the basic structure of an SQL statement. The simplest example looks like this:

```
SELECT *
FROM TBL_CUSTOMERS
```

Result:

	CUSTOMER_NO	FIRSTNAME	SURNAME	STREET	ZIP_CODE	CITY	GENDER	DATE_OF_BIRTH
1	1	Horst	Huber	Karolinenweg 11a	20357	Hamburg	M	01.05.75 00:00:00
2	2	Erika	Schmidt	Goethestraße 5	22512	Hamburg	F	05.10.85 00:00:00
3	3	Bert	Mueller	Schwedenweg 22	22123	Hamburg	m	03.02.79 00:00:00
4	4	Hubertus	Meyer-Huber	Hamburger Strasse 67	24106	Kiel	M	15.07.58 00:00:00
5	5	Hanna	von Bergmann	Werftstrasse 22	24145	Kiel	f	17.09.65 00:00:00
6	6	Tobias	Maier	Foerdeweg 2	26105	Flensburg	M	03.03.92 00:00:00
7	7	Fabian	Lindemann	Kieler Strasse 102	23809	Luebeck	m	01.09.73 00:00:00

The asterisk stands for all columns in the table. FROM <Table name> defines the table from which the data should be selected. If we only want to view specific columns, we can specify this by entering the column name. We can also use commas to select multiple columns:

```
SELECT CUSTOMER_NO,
       FIRST_NAME,
       SURNAME
FROM TBL_CUSTOMERS
```

This returns the following three columns:

Result:

	CUSTOMER_NO	FIRSTNAME	SURNAME
1	1	Horst	Huber
2	2	Erika	Schmidt
3	3	Bert	Mueller
4	4	Hubertus	Meyer-Huber
5	5	Hanna	von Bergmann
6	6	Tobias	Maier
7	7	Fabian	Lindemann

If we now query the only column CITY, the result would be:

Result:

CITY
1 Flensburg
2 Kiel
3 Luebeck
4 Hamburg

This returns the city for all datasets in the table. Using the keyword **DISTINCT** changes the result as follows:

```
SELECT DISTINCT CITY
FROM TBL_CUSTOMERS
```

Result:

CITY	GENDER
1 Hamburg	F
2 Flensburg	M
3 Luebeck	m
4 Hamburg	m
5 Hamburg	M
6 Kiel	M
7 Kiel	f

As you can see, using DISTINCT removes all duplicates and the different cities are only listed once. Here, all columns are always considered. This means that if you use DISTINCT for CITY and GENDER, the different combinations from the two columns will be displayed once. Duplicates in the combinations of the different column values are thus excluded.

```
-- Selecting distinct combinations

SELECT DISTINCT CITY, GENDER
FROM TBL_CUSTOMERS
```

Result:

Here, you have 2 rows for Hamburg and Kiel respectively since two columns have been selected and the duplicates eliminated for both CITY and GENDER.

You can use a double minus '--' to add **comments till the end of the line** in SQL statements. If you want to **comment in multiple lines** you have to put the comment between /* ..... */ .

Selecting rows (WHERE)

The next component of an SQL statement that you can use is the WHERE clause. This makes it possible to define the so-called filters, whereby you can select specific rows:

```
SELECT CUSTOMER_NO, FIRST_NAME, CITY
FROM TBL_CUSTOMER
WHERE CITY='Hamburg'
```

Result:

◊ CUSTOMER_NO	◊ FIRSTNAME	◊ SURNAME	◊ CITY
1	1 Horst	Huber	Hamburg
2	2 Erika	Schmidt	Hamburg
3	3 Bert	Mueller	Hamburg

This statement returns all rows with "Hamburg" as the city. In our example, this corresponds to the first three customers. There are different operators with which you can define filters:

Operator	Function
=	Equal
<>	Unequal
>	Greater than
<	Less than
>=	Greater or equal
<=	Less or equal
IS (NOT) NULL	Checks whether a column is (not) NULL
BETWEEN <value1> AND <value2>	Between <value1> and <value2>
IN (<value1>, <value2>, ...)	Contained in (...)
LIKE '.....'	Text similarity. % can be used as a placeholder for multiple arbitrary characters. _ is used as a placeholder for exactly one character.
<Operator> ANY (<value1>,...)	<Operator> can be: =, <, >, <>, <=, >= Oracle translates it to: <Operator> <value1> OR <Operator> <value2> OR ... In practice, it is mostly replaced by other comparisons and hence rather uncommon.
<Operator> ALL (<value1>,...)	<Operator> can be: =, <, >, <>, <=, >= Oracle translates it to: <Operator> <value1> AND <Operator> <value2> AND ... In practice, it is mostly replaced by other comparisons and hence rather uncommon.

Table 2: SQL comparison operators

For example, if you want to view all customers whose surname starts with an M, you could use the following SQL statement:

```
SELECT CUSTOMER_NO, FIRST_NAME, SURNAME
FROM TBL_CUSTOMERS
WHERE SURNAME LIKE 'M%'
```

Result:

◊ CUSTOMER_NO	◊ FIRSTNAME	◊ SURNAME
1	3 Bert	Mueller
2	4 Hubertus	Meyer-Huber
3	6 Tobias	Maier

'M%' means that the first letter in the string must be an M. The rest of the characters after that do not matter. This is achieved by the % sign. It is a placeholder for any number of characters. If you want a placeholder for exactly one character, you should use an underscore _.

Exercise 1: Display all products whose price is greater than 10€.

Exercise 2: Display all customers with their FIRST_NAME, SURNAME, and ZIP code if they come from ZIP code regions 24 + 25 (Tip: Do not use the LIKE operator).

Using calculations and functions

You can also perform calculations on the columns in the SELECT section and use them in filters as follows:

```
SELECT PRODUCT_NO, NAME, PRICE, PRICE/1.19 AS NET, PRICE/1.19*0.19 AS VAT
FROM TBL_PRODUCT
WHERE PRICE/1.19*0.19 > 2
```

Result:

◊ PRODUCT_NO	◊ NAME	◊ PRICE	◊ NET_PRICE	◊ VAT
1	1 Rumpsteak	20,95	17,6050420168067226890756302521008403361 3	3,34495798319327731092436974789915961
2	2 Grill platter	14,95	12,5630252100840336134453781512605042016 8	2,38697478991596638655462184873949571

As the example shows, you can also perform normal and well-known computational operations in SQL – both when using SELECT and the WHERE clause. In the above example, this has been used to only display rows with a VAT of more than 2 euros. You can use AS to rename columns. You can also use brackets.

The following math operators are hereby available:

Operator	Function
+, -, *, /	Addition, subtraction, multiplication, division with decimal places
mod (x,y)	Modulo division
^	Power

Table 3: Math operators

There are different functions that are implemented in databases. These can be used for rounding values, replacing characters in character strings, type conversion, computation with date values, etc. Below is a description of the most important functions:

Function/Syntax	Description
To_Date(<Value> [, <Format>])	Converts a string into a date. Here, you can specify a format string to define the structure of the value. For example, if you want to convert string '20120201' into a date, you must specify the format string 'YYYYMMDD'.

To_Char(<Value> [, <Format>])	Converts a date into a character string. You can specify a format string to define how the character string should appear. For example, you can easily convert date 01.02.2012 into '201202' using the format string 'YYYYMM'.
To_Number (<character string>)	Converts a character string into a number
Round (<number>, <figures>)	Rounds the number <number> commercially to <figures> figures
Substr (<Text>, <Start>, <no. of characters>)	Returns a text section from <Text>, starting from position <Start> and with <no. of characters> characters
Length (<Text>)	Returns the length of a character string in <Text>
InStr (<Text>, <character string>, <Start Pos.>)	Searches <character string> in <Text> starting from <Start Pos.> and returns the position
Replace (<Text>, <characters>, <new_characters>)	Replaces all <characters> characters with <new_characters> in <Text>
Concat (<Text1>, <Text2>, …)	Connects text 1 … n to a character string. Alternatively, you can also use the || operator.
LTrim/RTrim (<Text> [, <characters>])	Trims all <characters> characters to the left/right of <Text>. If no characters are specified, empty spaces are removed.
NVL (<field>, <null_value_characters>)	Replaces NULL values in <field> with <null_value_characters>
ADD_MONTHS (<date>, <months<)	Adds <months> months to <date> and returns the corresponding date
LAST_DAY (<date>)	Returns the last day of the month from <date>
UPPER / LOWER (<text>)	Converts all characters from <Text> to upper/lower case
LPad/RPad(<text>, <width> [, <characters>])	Fills string <text> with <characters> up to <width> characters. If no characters are specified, the string is filled with empty spaces.
ABS (<number>)	Returns the absolute number
SYSDATE / SYSTIMESTAMP	Returns the current system date/current system stamp (i.e. date and time)
TRUNC (<number>, <count>)	Truncates the <number> up to <count> decimal places. It is not rounded. If you do not specify the <count>, the number is cut off at the decimal point.

Table 4: Standard functions in Oracle

You can find a comprehensive overview of all possible format string components at: http://docs.oracle.com/cd/B28359_01/olap.111/b28126/dml_commands_1029.htm#OLADM780.

You can use the functions both in the SELECT as well as the WHERE section of an SQL statement, thus allowing you further filter options:

SELECT CUSTOMER_NO, FIRST_NAME, SURNAME, Date_of_Birth
FROM TBL_CUSTOMERS
WHERE to_number(to_char(Date_of_Birth, 'YYYY'))>=1980

Result:

	CUSTOMER_NO	FIRSTNAME	SURNAME	DATE_OF_BIRTH
1	2	Erika	Schmidt	05.10.85 00:00:00
2	6	Tobias	Maier	03.03.92 00:00:00

As you can see, one can also combine multiple functions. This example selects all customers born after 1980. The string function can then be used to filter out all male customers:

SELECT FIRST_NAME, SURNAME, GENDER
FROM TBL_CUSTOMERS
WHERE UPPER(GENDER)='M'

Result:

	FIRSTNAME	SURNAME	GENDER
1	Horst	Huber	M
2	Bert	Mueller	m
3	Hubertus	Meyer-Huber	M
4	Tobias	Maier	M
5	Fabian	Lindemann	m

Why use the UPPER function? An uppercase M and a lowercase m could have been used interchangeably for the gender. Alternatively, you can also do the same using the 'IN' operator: IN('M', 'm').

Exercise 3: Select all customers who celebrate their birthday in the first quarter of a year.

Exercise 4: Use SQL functions to display all customers whose first name starts with an F (do not use the LIKE operator)!

Exercise 5: Use SQL functions to select all customers whose surname end with 'mann' (do not use the LIKE operator). Tip: substr + length

Combining multiple filters

It is often necessary to select datasets based on multiple criteria. For example, you might want to view all female customers who were born after 1970:

```
SELECT CUSTOMER_NO, FIRST_NAME, SURNAME, GENDER, DATE_OF_BIRTH
FROM TBL_CUSTOMERS
WHERE to_number( to_char(DATE_OF_BIRTH, 'YYYY'))>=1970
AND GENDER IN('F', 'f')
```

Result:

	CUSTOMER_NO	FIRSTNAME	SURNAME	GENDER	DATE_OF_BIRTH
1	2	Erika	Schmidt	F	05.10.85 00:00:00

You can combine multiple filters using **AND**. This means that both conditions must be met for the required dataset to be returned. The second dataset is not displayed in this case since the Date_of_Birth does not meet the requirements.

You can also combine conditions using **OR**. This means that the dataset is returned if A or B is met:

```
SELECT FIRST_NAME, SURNAME, GENDER, DATE_OF_BIRTH
FROM TBL_CUSTOMERS
WHERE GENDER IN('F', 'f')
OR to_number( to_char(DATE_OF_BIRTH, 'YYYY'))>=1970
```

Result:

	FIRSTNAME	SURNAME	GENDER	DATE_OF_BIRTH
1	Horst	Huber	M	01.05.75 00:00:00
2	Erika	Schmidt	F	05.10.85 00:00:00
3	Bert	Mueller	m	03.02.79 00:00:00
4	Hanna	von Bergmann	f	17.09.65 00:00:00
5	Tobias	Maier	M	03.03.92 00:00:00
6	Fabian	Lindemann	m	01.09.73 00:00:00

This returns all customers who are female or customers who were born after 1970. The whole thing becomes more complex if you combine AND and OR. In this case, the AND operator takes precedence over the OR operator:

```
SELECT FIRST_NAME, SURNAME, CITY, GENDER
FROM TBL_CUSTOMERS
WHERE CITY='Hamburg' OR CITY='Kiel' AND GENDER IN('M', 'm')
```

Result:

	FIRSTNAME	SURNAME	CITY	GENDER
1	Horst	Huber	Hamburg	M
2	Erika	Schmidt	Hamburg	F
3	Bert	Mueller	Hamburg	m
4	Hubertus	Meyer-Huber	Kiel	M

Sometimes you need to use brackets depending on what you want to evaluate. According to the statement defined above, the query returns customers who live in Hamburg (whether male or female) or male customers from Kiel.

If you want to view male customers who come from Kiel or Hamburg, you must extend the SQL as follows:

```
SELECT FIRST_NAME, SURNAME, CITY, GENDER
FROM TBL_CUSTOMERS
WHERE (CITY='Hamburg' OR CITY='Kiel') AND GENDER IN('M', 'm')
```

Result:

	FIRSTNAME	SURNAME	CITY	GENDER
1	Horst	Huber	Hamburg	M
2	Bert	Mueller	Hamburg	m
3	Hubertus	Meyer-Huber	Kiel	M

The dataset "Erika Schmidt" is now excluded since the datasets to be returned must now fulfill the following conditions:
1. male
2. from Kiel or Hamburg

This was achieved by using brackets. The condition (CITY='Hamburg' OR CITY='KIEL') is evaluated first. The result is then analyzed to see which of the customers are male.

In the context of AND and OR, we also have the NOT operator. For example, this can be used to check which customers do not come from Kiel, Flensburg, or Lübeck:

```
SELECT FIRST_NAME, SURNAME, CITY
FROM TBL_CUSTOMERS
WHERE CITY NOT IN ('Hamburg', 'Flensburg', 'Lübeck')
```

Result:

	FIRSTNAME	SURNAME	CITY
1	Hubertus	Meyer-Huber	Kiel
2	Hanna	von Bergmann	Kiel

Exercise 6: Select all products with product group 1 and a price greater than 15€.

Exercise 7: Select all products with a VAT value <0.75€ or >2€ from product groups 1, 2, or 4. Make sure to display all columns of the product table and additionally display the VAT (VAT rate: 19%).

Sorting results
You can also use different criteria to sort the displays query results, e.g., based on the ZIP code:

```
SELECT CUSTOMER_NO, FIRST_NAME, SURNAME, ZIP_code
```

```
FROM TBL_CUSTOMERS
ORDER BY PLZ ASC
```

Result:

CUSTOMER_NO	FIRSTNAME	SURNAME	ZIP_CODE
1	1 Horst	Huber	20357
2	3 Bert	Mueller	22123
3	2 Erika	Schmidt	22512
4	7 Fabian	Lindemann	23809
5	4 Hubertus	Meyer-Huber	24106
6	5 Hanna	von Bergmann	24145
7	6 Tobias	Maier	26105

Below is another example on sorting results:

```
SELECT CUSTOMER_NO, FIRST_NAME, SURNAME, CITY
FROM TBL_CUSTOMERS
ORDER BY 4 DESC, 1 ASC
```

Result:

CUSTOMER_NO	FIRSTNAME	SURNAME	CITY
1	7 Fabian	Lindemann	Luebeck
2	4 Hubertus	Meyer-Huber	Kiel
3	5 Hanna	von Bergmann	Kiel
4	1 Horst	Huber	Hamburg
5	2 Erika	Schmidt	Hamburg
6	3 Bert	Mueller	Hamburg
7	6 Tobias	Maier	Flensburg

As you can see, you can use **ASC** or **DESC** to define the direction in which you want to sort the data. Sorting columns can be specified either by name or position. You can combine multiple sorting criteria using commas.

NULLS FIRST and **NULLS LAST** enables you to place zeroes at the start or end of a list during sorting. The rest is then sorted as described.

One brief topic to conclude this chapter: Oracle has a table called DUAL. This has exactly one dataset. This small table can be helpful at times since in Oracle, you must specify a table in the FROM clause in Oracle. For example, if I want to quickly try out a function, I can use the following statement:

```
SELECT SYSDATE
FROM dual;
```

This returns exactly one value, i.e. the system date in this case.

Exercises

1) Generate a list of all female customers from Hamburg.

2) Your driver, Liese, is always too slow getting to customers. As a result, most pizzas are cold and there have been many complaints from these customers. In order to offer all customers who were served by Liese a free tiramisu as compensation, you need a list of all orders from the 1st quarter of 2013 that were delivered by Liese (employee no.). No pick-ups. (Tip: First get Liese's employee no. in TBL_EMPLOYEES and then use the query)

3) Display all customers who are older than 40 years. In addition, make sure to also display their respective age. (Tip: You can also subtract date fields)

4) Select all orders (order no.) with at least two pieces of products 1...5 or at least three pieces of products 6... 15. (Tip: Use TBL_ORDER_POS)

5) Create a report showing the orders for customers from Hamburg in the 1st quarter of 2013. (Tip: First look up the relevant customers in TBL_CUSTOMERS and then use the corresponding customer no. in the query)

6) Which customers were served by seller Emil Iversen and driver Liese Müller or by seller Emil Iversen and driver Peter Peters in February or August 2013? Only use the AND, OR, NOT operators.

7) Display all customers whose street name contains 'weg'. Do not use the LIKE operator.

4   Querying multiple tables

We now know how to create simple queries in a table. However, most applications require access to multiple tables. Looking at the customers or products alone is somehow boring. We want to know where and how often the products were sold. For us to be able to do this, this chapter describes the different 'Join' types for relational databases.

Cross product

The simplest way to query data from multiple tables is by simply writing a second table in the FROM clause. However, in most cases, this does not return what you want. This is because, in this case, relational databases combine all datasets from table A with all datasets from table B. For large tables, this can result in very large outputs that can push your database performance to its limits.

However, you also have cases where cross products can be useful. Let us first look at the syntax for a cross product:

```
SELECT
        TBL_CUSTOMERS.CUSTOMER_NO,
        TBL_CUSTOMERS.SURNAME,
        TBL_PRODUCT_GROUP.PRODUCT_GROUP_NO AS PG_NO,
        TBL_PRODUCT_GROUP.NAME AS PG_NAME
FROM TBL_CUSTOMERS, TBL_PRODUCT_GROUP
ORDER BY 1,3
```

Result:

	CUSTOMER_NO	SURNAME	PG_NR	PG_BEZ
1	1	Huber	1	Meat dishes
2	1	Huber	2	Pizzas
3	1	Huber	3	Pasta
4	1	Huber	4	Drinks
5	1	Huber	5	Desserts
6	1	Huber	6	Others
7	2	Schmidt	1	Meat dishes
8	2	Schmidt	2	Pizzas
9	2	Schmidt	3	Pasta
10	2	Schmidt	4	Drinks
11	2	Schmidt	5	Desserts

As you have seen, you only need to specify the tables that you want to define a cross product for in the FROM clause. You can also do the same in SELECT and specify which columns should be taken from which table using the following syntax: *<Table name> . <Column name>*
The above example also shows the effect of the cross product. We have exactly seven datasets in TBL_CUSTOMERS, five in TBL_PRODUCT_GROUP. In total, each dataset from TBL_CUSTOMERS will be combined with every dataset from TBL_PRODUCT_GROUP, resulting in 35 datasets.

Inner joins

Contrary to the cross product, inner joins links the two tables via one or more columns. This is illustrated in the example of the inner join between products and order positions:

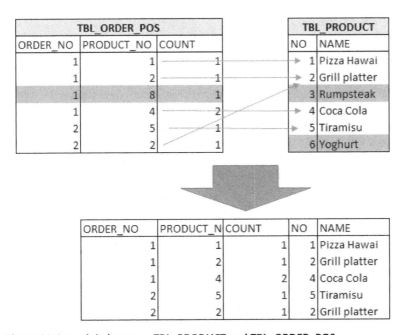

Figure 11: Inner join between TBL_PRODUCT and TBL_ORDER_POS

The two tables should be linked via the PRODUCT_NO. To do this, the database searches for datasets in which the values are identical in the link columns. These two datasets are then merged to get the resulting set. The links are indicated by the thin blue arrows. The red arrows have no correspondence in the other table and are therefore excluded from the resulting datasets.

Let us look at another simple example and assume we want to know the product group to which our products belong. Here, we have the product group number in the product table. However, this number is not exactly meaningful for most users and it would be better to also display the name of the product group from the product group table. For us to do this, we must link TBL_PRODUCT with TBL_PRODUCT_GROUP. We can do this via the PRODUCT_GROUP_NO column since, according to the data model, this column provides a link between the two tables.

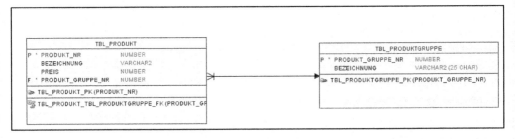

Figure 12: Section of product and product group from the data model

The following SQL creates a link between the two tables and returns all columns:

```
SELECT *
FROM TBL_PRODUCT prd
        JOIN TBL_PRODUCT_GROUP grp
        ON prd.PRODUCT_GROUP_NO=grp.PRODUCT_GROUP_NO
WHERE grp.PRODUCT_GROUP_NO IN(1,5)
```

Result:

PRODUCT_NO	NAME	PRICE	PRODUCT_GROUP_NO	TURNOVER_PRODUCT	TURNOVER_ANTEIL	PRODUCT_GROUP_NO_1	NAME_1
1	1 Rumpsteak	20,95	1	4546,15	0,23	1	Meat dishes
2	2 Grill platter	14,95	1	3303,95	0,16	1	Meat dishes
3	14 Fruit salad	3	5	696	0,03	5	Desserts
4	15 Tiramisu	4	5	832	0,04	5	Desserts
5	16 Yoghurt	(null)	5	(null)	(null)	5	Desserts

This lets us view the product groups 1 and 5 with their products. The link is established using *<Table 1> JOIN <Table 2> ON <Conditions>*. Prd and grp are called table aliases. They allow us to give the tables different, simpler names and then access the columns. In the above example, the DBMS first goes through all columns of the product table while checking the product_group_no in each row. The database then uses this number to link to the product_group table and selects all datasets with this number. The fields of the dataset from TBL_PRODUCT and TBL_PRODUCT_GROUP are added to a new, resulting dataset. This is done for each row in the product table. In the end, only the datasets that belong to product group 1 or 5 are displayed. If you do not limit the fields, all fields from both tables are taken. For fields that have the same name (e.g., PRODUCT_GROUP_NO), the DBMS automatically adds a number at the end to make them unique.

In the case of an inner join, only the datasets that have a corresponding dataset in both table A and table B are returned. Datasets that do not have a referenced dataset in table B are excluded from the result. This is illustrated in the example below. There is no product assigned to product group 6 (=others):

```
SELECT grp.NAME AS GROUP, prd.NAME AS PROD
FROM TBL_PRODUCT prd
        JOIN TBL_PRODUCT_GROUP grp
        ON prd.PRODUCT_GROUP_NO=grp.PRODUCT_GROUP_NO
WHERE grp.PRODUCT_GROUP_NO IN(5,6)
```

Result:

GROUP_NAME	PROD
1 Desserts	Fruit salad
2 Desserts	Tiramisu
3 Desserts	Yoghurt

Let's now look at a small effect with joins and use it to manipulate the data in the product group table:

```
ALTER TABLE TBL_PRODUCT DISABLE CONSTRAINT FK_PROD_PROD_GROUP;

ALTER TABLE TBL_PRODUCT_GROUP DISABLE CONSTRAINT PK_PROD_GROUP;

INSERT INTO TBL_PRODUCT_GROUP VALUES (1, 'Test group');

COMMIT;

SELECT *
FROM TBL_PRODUCT prd
     JOIN TBL_PRODUCT_GROUP grp
     ON prd.PRODUCT_GROUP_NO=grp.PRODUCT_GROUP_NO
WHERE grp.PRODUCT_GROUP_NO=1;
```

Result:

	PRODUCT_NO	NAME	PRICE	PRODUCT_GROUP_NO	PRODUCT_GROUP_NO_1	NAME_1
1	1	Rumpsteak	20,95	1	1	Testgruppe
2	1	Rumpsteak	20,95	1	1	Meat dishes
3	2	Grill platter	14,95	1	1	Testgruppe
4	2	Grill platter	14,95	1	1	Meat dishes

What just happened here? There are two entries for the same PRODUCT_GROUP_NO in the product group table, i.e. 1 meat dishes and 1 test group: With join, all datasets from TBL_PRODUCT_GROUP are taken if the join condition is met. Since both groups have 1 as the number, they both fulfill the criterion and are therefore returned. Thus, the database combines every product from group no. 1 with both groups and hence result in duplicates. This is a very common phenomenon, especially if you have deactivated foreign key constraints (which we have already covered with the ALTER commands).

Next, we will use the following brief script to restore to the former state:

```
DELETE TBL_PRODUCT_GROUP WHERE NAME='Test group';

COMMIT;

ALTER TABLE TBL_PRODUCT_GROUP ENABLE CONSTRAINT PK_PROD_GROUP;

ALTER TABLE TBL_PRODUCT ENABLE CONSTRAINT FK_PROD_PROD_GROUP;
```

Exercise 1: Create a query that shows you the name of the customers who placed an order in February 2013.

You can also create queries for more than two tables. This basically works the same way as with just two tables. The only difference is that each additional table must be added using a separate join in the query.

Exercise 2: Which drivers (no., name) delivered to customer 'Müller' in April 2013?

Exercise 3: Which products (name, price) were purchased by customers from Kiel in the 2nd quarter of 2013?

Sometimes, you also need to create joins over more than one column. The additional join conditions (join columns) are linked using the AND operator in the ON clause.

Left / Right / Full outer joins

Whereas the inner join only returns datasets with references in table A (left table) and table B (right table), the outer join returns all datasets from one table and, if the join conditions are met, the corresponding datasets from table B as well. If there is no correspondence in table B, the fields from table B are filled with NULL.

```
SELECT grp.NAME AS GROUP, prd.NAME AS PROD
FROM TBL_PRODUCT_GROUP grp
        LEFT JOIN TBL_PRODUCT prd ON grp.PRODUCT_GROUP_NO=prd.PRODUCT_GROUP_NO
WHERE grp.PRODUCT_GROUP_NO IN (5,6)
ORDER BY 1,2
```

Result:

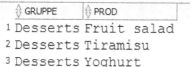

	GRUPPE	PROD
1	Desserts	Fruit salad
2	Desserts	Tiramisu
3	Desserts	Yoghurt
4	Others	(null)

Compared to the same SQL statement for inner joins (see page 29), group 6(=others) is now also included in the result. The only difference is the small word, LEFT before JOIN. This converts the inner join into a LEFT OUTER JOIN, i.e. an outer join with the leading table on the left-hand side (to the left of the join). All datasets from this table as well as the matching ones from the table on the right-hand side are taken. Here, the only matching products are in the desserts group. You can use outer joins to easily find out which datasets are not used in other tables. To do this, add a WHERE filter that filters the NULL values in the join column of the table on the right. A RIGHT OUTER JOIN works in the same way, except that the leading table, i.e. the table from which all datasets are taken, is to the RIGHT of JOIN.

Below is a graphical illustration of the outer join:

TBL_PRODUCT	
NO	NAME
1	Pizza Hawai
2	Grill platter
3	Rumpsteak
4	Coca Cola
5	Tiramisu
6	Yoghurt

TBL_ORDER_POS		
ORDER_NO	PRODUCT_NO	COUNT
1	1	1
1	2	1
1	8	1
1	4	2
2	5	1
2	2	1

NO	NAME	ORDER_NO	PRODUCT_N	COUNT
1	Pizza Hawai	1	1	1
2	Grill platter	1	2	1
2	Grill platter	2	2	1
3	Rumpsteak	<null>	<null>	<null>
4	Coca Cola	1	4	2
5	Tiramisu	2	5	1
6	Yoghurt	<null>	<null>	<null>

Figure 13: Outer join between TBL_PRODUCT (leading) and TBL_ORDER_POS

Here as well, attempts are made to link the datasets of both tables. The linking columns are compared with one another and in the case of similarities, the corresponding datasets combined. The figure shows the links between the thin blue arrows. In this case, only the one dataset in TBL_ORDER_POS is excluded since TBL_PRODUCT is defined as the leading table and hence all its datasets are taken. Datasets 3+6 in the product table do not have correspondents. They are therefore filled with <null> in the result set with table TBL_ORDER_POS.

Exercise 4: Which products were not sold?

Outer joins and inner joins can be used in queries simultaneously. We also have the so-called full outer joins. Here, all datasets from both tables are taken and either combined in the case of intersections or filled with NULL if there are no intersections.

Exercises

1) Which driver delivered to which customer in April 2013?

2) Display the different products that customer 'Maier' ordered in April 2013.

3) Which customers from Hamburg ordered 'Rump steak' in February 2013?

4) Which employees have not yet delivered any orders?

5) Which orders (order no.) include products from the 'meat dishes'?

5 Grouping and aggregation

Aggregate functions

So far, all our queries have returned individual datasets. For example, we have managed to view all orders placed by customers from a specific city, but not the respective sums for each city. To do so, we need to calculate the sum of the individual sets from the different cities. This is called aggregating. There are different aggregate functions for this purpose. In our example, it is e.g. advisable to simply sum up all the individual sales. You could also view the largest, smallest, or average sales. Below is a list of available aggregate functions:

Aggregate function	Description
SUM (<value>)	Sum of the values. Only available for numeric columns.
AVG (<value>)	Average of the values. Only available for numeric columns.
MIN (<value>)	Minimum value. Also available for text and date values.
MAX (<value>)	Maximum value. Also available for text and date values.
Count (<value>)	Number of values. Also available for text and date values.
Count (DISTINCT <value>)	Number of different values. Also available for text and date values.
Count(*)	Number of datasets.

Table 5: Aggregate functions

Let us take a simple example. If we want to know how many servings of Spaghetti Bolognese were sold in March 2013, we can use the following SQL:

```
SELECT SUM(bpos.COUNT)
FROM TBL_ORDER best
        JOIN TBL_ORDER_POS bpos ON best.ORDER_NO=bpos.ORDER_NO
WHERE bpos.PRODUCT_NO=8
AND to_char(best.ORDER_DATE, 'YYYYMM')='201303'
```

Result:

	SUM(BPOS.COUNT)
1	12

According to SQL, there were two servings. We can verify this by simply replacing SUM(bpos.COUNT) with bpos.* in the above query:

Result:

	ORDER_NO	ORDER_DATE	CUSTOMER_NO	DRIVER_NO	SALES_AGENT_NO	ORDER_NO_1	PRODUCT_NO	COUNT
1	30	15.03.13 00:00:00	2	2	6	30	8	3
2	60	08.03.13 00:00:00	3	5	6	60	8	2
3	114	11.03.13 00:00:00	2	4	6	114	8	1
4	120	05.03.13 00:00:00	2	1	7	120	8	2
5	130	21.03.13 00:00:00	5	1	7	130	8	3
6	155	22.03.13 00:00:00	7	3	6	155	8	1

As you can see, there are two datasets in the table TBL_ORDER_POS that fulfil the conditions, each with a count of 1 and hence a sum of 2. However, instead of 6 individual datasets, we have received a single summarized dataset.

Exercise 1: How many cooks are there?

Exercise 2: What is the average price of all products?

Groupings using GROUP BY

Sometimes, you are not just interested in the total sum. You may also want to find out the individual sums for different categories, e.g., sum per product or minimum and maximum price per product group. You can do this using the so-called groupings. The aggregate function is then applied to the corresponding group. Groupings are defined using the GROUP BY statement. Here is an example:

Nr	Bezeichnung	Anzahl
1	Rumpsteak	3
1	Rumpsteak	4
1	Rumpsteak	5
...		
2	Grillteller	3
2	Grillteller	3
2	Grillteller	3
...		

Nr	Bezeichnung	SUM(Anzahl)
1	Rumpsteak	217
2	Grillteller	221
3	Pizza Salami	211
...		

```
SELECT p.PRODUKT_NR,
       p.BEZEICHNUNG,
       bp.ANZAHL
FROM TBL_PRODUKT p
  JOIN TBL_BESTELLUNG_POS bp ON ....
ORDER BY 1
```

```
SELECT p.PRODUKT_NR,
       p.BEZEICHNUNG,
       SUM(bp.ANZAHL)
FROM TBL_PRODUKT p
  JOIN TBL_BESTELLUNG_POS bp ON ....
GROUP BY p.PRODUKT_NR, p.BEZEICHNUNG
ORDER BY 1
```

On the left-hand side, we have the sales numbers of products and product names. For every order item (i.e. each different product in a purchase order), there is a dataset in the TBL_ORDER_POS table. We are now going to create a query for a grouping based on the product. This is illustrated on the right-hand side and shows all columns that belong to the product. In this case, we have the product no. and product name. As a result, we get the sum of all associated datasets from the purchase orders in each row.

The following condition must always be fulfilled when working with aggregate and grouping functions:
> *Every column in SELECT must use an aggregate function (i.e. SUM, MAX, MIN, AVG, ...) or*
> *GROUP BY.*

If this is not fulfilled, corresponding error messages are displayed. Aggregate functions may only appear in SELECT but not in GROUP BY. In addition, when creating queries through aggregation and grouping, you should always consider the level at which you want to find the sums. In this case, no other columns that result in grouping at a more detailed level may be used.

For example, if you want to create a list showing all product groups and their average prices, you cannot use elements from the products in the grouping columns. This would create groups at a product

35

level and you would therefore return a row for each product. However, you can use columns from the product within the aggregate function since these columns are aggregated by the aggregate function.

Below is another example of groupings and aggregation:

```
SELECT grp.NAME AS GROUP_NAME, Count(*) AS AMT, MIN(prd.PRICE), MAX(prd.PRICE)
FROM TBL_PRODUCT prd
        JOIN TBL_PRODUCTGROUP grp
        ON prd.PRODUCT_GROUP_NO=grp.PRODUCT_GROUP_NO
GROUP BY grp.NAME
```

Result:

GROUP_NAME	ANZ	MIN(PRD.PRICE)	MAX(PRD.PRICE)
1 Desserts	3	3	4
2 Pasta	3	4,5	4,5
3 Pizzas	5	5,6	6,95
4 Meat dishes	2	14,95	20,95
5 Drinks	3	1,75	2

We have calculated the corresponding number of products as well as the minimum and maximum values for our 5 product groups. Group 6 is not included in the result due to the use of an inner join. Otherwise, we can see that in SQL the grouping is only done using the name of the product group, i.e. a row is generated for every product group name.

Exercise 3: Generate a list showing all orders with their respective sales (count * price).

Exercise 4: Which city had the most sales in the 1st quarter of 2013? Create a list of the cities showing their total sales, sorted in descending order.

Selecting groups for the result (HAVING)

Sometimes, it might be necessary to exclude certain groups based on their aggregates. This is done using the HAVING clause. For example, you can use this clause to list down all products with total sales of €3000 or more:

```
SELECT
        prd.PRODUCT_NO AS NO,
        prd.NAME AS PRODUCT,
        SUM(bpos.COUNT) AS VK_ITEMS,
        SUM(prd.PRICE*bpos.COUNT) AS SALES
FROM TBL_PRODUCT prd
        JOIN TBL_ORDER_POS bpos ON prd.PRODUCT_NO=bpos.PRODUCT_NO
GROUP BY prd.PRODUCT_NO, prd.NAME
HAVING SUM(prd.PRICE*bpos.COUNT)>=3000
```

Result:

NO	PRODUCT	SALES_AMOUNT	TURNOVER
1	2 Grill platter	221	3303,95
2	1 Rumpsteak	217	4546,15

This filters out all groups with sales < €3000.

Exercise 5: Create a list showing product groups with an average price of more than €6.

Exercises

1) Which driver delivered the most pizzas?

2) Which customer placed the most orders in the 2nd quarter of 2013 and how many?

3) Which product was the least popular (based on the sales figures) among customers in March 2013?

4) What were the sales per product group and per month in the period between March 2013 and May 2013?

5) Create a ranking of the products based on the sales from the 1st quarter of 2013. You should also include products that have not been sold so far.

6) How many different customers did every driver deliver to? How many deliveries did every driver manage?

7) Which city had the highest average sales per order? Which city had the lowest?

8) Create a list of all sellers showing their sales and commissions. Also, list down those without any sales or commissions. Sort the results by commissions in descending order.

6   Subqueries

In chapter 5, we learnt the different join types that we can use to query data from multiple tables. In this chapter, we will be dealing with another variant, the so-called subqueries. This involves combining two queries, whereby one of the queries is based on the results of the other.

Nested queries

Sometimes, you want to calculate specific things and then evaluate the result further. In such a case, you can use nested queries where a query accesses the result of another query instead of re-accessing the table. In the example below, the first query first lists down the number of products per product group whereas the other finds the average number of products:

```
SELECT AVG(COUNT)
FROM (
        SELECT PRODUCT_GROUP_NO, Count(PRODUCT_NO) AS COUNT
        FROM TBL_PRODUCT
        GROUP BY PRODUCT_GROUP_NO
)
```

Result:

	AVG(COUNT)
1	3,2

First, the initial query returns the following result:

	PRODUCT_GROUP_NO	COUNT
1	1	2
2	2	5
3	4	3
4	5	3
5	3	3

Next, the superordinate query takes these 5 values and calculates their average.

You can therefore use queries in the place of tables. You can also assign an alias to queries and join them with other queries or tables. Here is an example: We need a list of all products and their total sales. This should then be used to calculate the respective product group sales and then determine the sales share of each product in the respective product group.

```
SELECT products.*,
        prod_group.SALES_PG,
        round(products. SALES/prod_group.SALES_PG*100,1) AS RATIO

FROM (
        SELECT p.PRODUCT_NO,
              p.NAME AS PROD_NAME,
```

```
            p.PRODUCT_GROUP_NO AS PG_NO,
            SUM(bp.COUNT*p.PRICE) AS SALES
      FROM TBL_ORDER_POS bp
         JOIN TBL_PRODUCT p ON bp.PRODUCT_NO=p.PRODUCT_NO
         GROUP BY p.PRODUCT_NO, p.NAME, p.PRODUCT_GROUP_NO
      ) products

JOIN (
         SELECT p.PRODUCT_GROUP_NO,
                SUM(bp.COUNT*p.PRICE) AS SALES_PG
         FROM TBL_ORDER_POS bp
            JOIN TBL_PRODUCT p ON bp.PRODUCT_NO=p.PRODUCT_NO
            GROUP BY p.PRODUCT_GROUP_NO
      ) prod_group

ON products.PG_NO=prod_group.PRODUCT_GROUP_NO

ORDER BY 3, 1
```

Result:

	PRODUCT_NO	PROD_NAME	PG_NO	SALES	SALES_PG	RATIO
1	1	Rumpsteak	1	4546,15	7850,1	57,9
2	2	Grill platter	1	3303,95	7850,1	42,1
3	3	Pizza Salami	2	1181,6	6603,1	17,9
4	4	Pizza Hawai	2	1250,5	6603,1	18,9
5	5	Pizza Thunfisch	2	1195,6	6603,1	18,1
6	6	Pizza Spezial	2	1612,4	6603,1	24,4
7	7	Pizza Vital	2	1363	6603,1	20,6
8	8	Spagetti Bolognese	3	873	2808	31,1
9	9	Lasagne	3	873	2808	31,1
10	10	Tagliatelle Carbonara	3	1062	2808	37,8
11	11	Coke 0,331	4	348,25	1308,25	26,6

In this example, we have used two subqueries. The yellow one calculates the sales per product whereas the blue one calculates the sales per product group. In the yellow query, we still have the product group number, with which we can later link these two queries.

Each of these subqueries can be executed on its own, then using the main query instead of tables. Both subqueries are linked to the main query using brackets (….) and are assigned corresponding alias names. For subqueries, you must always use an alias name since they of course initially have no name in the system (unlike tables, which have a unique name in the database). The linking is done just as if one were linking two tables. In this regard, the linking columns from both subqueries must be specified in the ON clause.

The database first checks if there is a corresponding dataset in the product group subquery for every dataset in the product subquery (i.e. for every dataset per product) and assigns any findings accordingly. We therefore get the product group sales assigned to the respective products and can now also calculate the corresponding sales shares.

In summary, we have seen that you can also use queries in queries instead of tables. The columns from SELECT in the subquery correspond to the column in the tables. One can thus use these for links, filters, and calculations just as with tables. Now a small exercise on this.

Exercise 1: Create a list of all customers with their total sales. Calculate the sales share of each customer in the total shares from his/her place of residence.

Exercise 2: Create a query that determines the average product price for each product group. Create a link between this query and the product table to only display products whose price is above the average of their product group.

Subqueries and the IN operator

We now want to list down the products groups that are not assigned any product. We can either do this using an outer join construct (like in chapter 5) or with a subquery:

```
SELECT PRODUCT_GROUP_NO AS NO, NAME AS GROUP_NAME
FROM TBL_PRODUCT_GROUP
WHERE PRODUCT_GROUP_NO NOT IN (
        SELECT DISTINCT PRODUCT_GROUP_NO
        FROM TBL_PRODUCT
)
```

Result:

NO	GROUP_NAME
1	6 Others

Here, we have used two SQLs. The statement within the IN operator returns a list of the product group numbers used in the product table. This result is then used as the content of the list within the IN statement in the product table. This returns the product groups whose number is not in the list returned by the second SQL.

You can also use more complex SQLs as expressions within the IN operator. Here, the most important thing is for them to only have one column in SELECT.

Exercise 3: Which orders (order no.) include products whose price is > €8 ? Use subqueries.

Exercise 4: Which orders (order no.) include products from product groups whose average price is > €6 ?

Subqueries in the WHERE clause

In some cases, you might need to calculate a certain value and then use it as a comparison value in filters. For instance, let's assume you wanted to list down all products with prices higher than the average price of all products. To do this, you would need a subquery that first calculates the average price of all products and then compares the prices in the price table with this value:

```
SELECT PRODUCT_NO, NAME, PRICE
FROM TBL_PRODUCT
WHERE PRICE>= (
        SELECT AVG(PRICE)
        FROM TBL_PRODUCT
)
```

Result:

	PRODUCT_NO	NAME	PRICE
1	1	Rumpsteak	20,95
2	2	Grill platter	14,95
3	6	Pizza Spezial	6,95

With the average price of all products being €6.18, we have three products that are more expensive than this average. For these subqueries, it is important to make sure that only a single value is returned. Otherwise, if your initial query returns several values, it would be unclear which comparison value should be used by the database.

Exercise 5: Which employees earn less than 75% of the average salary?

Linking a subquery with the main query

In exercise 2, you should first determine the average price per product group and then link the result to the product table to list down only the products whose price is greater than or equal to the average price of their respective product group. You can also do this using a subquery that is linked to a filter:

```
SELECT  grp.NAME AS GROUP,
        PRODUCT_NO AS NO,
        p_main.NAME AS PRODUCT,
        PRICE,
        (
                SELECT AVG(PRICE)
                FROM TBL_PRODUCT p_sub
                WHERE p_sub PRODUCT_GROUP_NO=p_main PRODUCT_GROUP_NO
        ) AS  GRP_AVG

FROM TBL_PRODUCT p_main
        JOIN TBL_PRODUCT_GROUP grp
        ON p_main.PRODUCT_GROUP_NO=grp.PRODUCT_GROUP_NO

WHERE p_main.PRICE>=(

        SELECT AVG(PRICE)
        FROM TBL_PRODUCT p_sub
        WHERE p_sub PRODUCT_GROUP_NO=p_main PRODUCT_GROUP_NO
)
```

Result:

	GROUP_NAME	NO	PRODUCT	PRICE	GRP_AVG
1	Meat dishes	1	Rumpsteak	20,95	17,95
2	Pizzas	6	Pizza Spezial	6,95	6,11
3	Pasta	8	Spagetti Bolognese	4,5	4,5
4	Pasta	9	Lasagne	4,5	4,5
5	Pasta	10	Tagliatelle Carbonara	4,5	4,5
6	Drinks	12	Beer Holsten 0,5l	2	1,91666666666666666666666666666666666667
7	Drinks	13	Water 1,5l with gas	2	1,91666666666666666666666666666666666667
8	Desserts	15	Tiramisu	4	3,5

In this query, we have combined several techniques that we have learnt so far (joins, grouping, subquery). In the subquery, we have something new. We use it to determine the average value for a specific product group. We have first applied a filter to the product group, which is based on the product group of the superordinate query. Oracle therefore goes through the datasets of the product table in the superordinate query and executes the subquery for each dataset. Here, the respective value of the product group of the superordinate query is used as a filter criterion for the subquery.

Exercise 6: Create a list showing employees who earn 20% more than the average in their employee group (drivers, sellers, etc.). (Tip: You should calculate three average salaries (for each employee group) and compare with the employees in that group.)

Subqueries using the EXISTS operator

The EXISTS operator checks if there is a valid value for a specific dataset. This requires linking the main query to the subquery:

```
SELECT *
FROM TBL_PRODUCT_GROUP grp
WHERE NOT EXISTS (
    SELECT 1
    FROM TBL_PRODUCT prd
    WHERE prd.PRODUCT_GROUP_NO=grp.PRODUCT_GROUP_NO
)
```

Result:

	PRODUCT_GROUP_NO	NAME
1	6	Others

The subquery is performed on every dataset returned by the main query, with a filter based on the product group number in the main query. If there are any products belonging to this group, the subquery returns the corresponding values, the EXISTS operator returns "TRUE", and the corresponding dataset is included in the result. In our example, we have used NOT EXISTS to determine the datasets without a result in the subquery and that are therefore not used in this product group since they do not have corresponding products.

Subqueries in DML operations

You can also use subqueries in INSERT, UPDATE, and DELETE statements. Let us look at one simple example for each of these cases.

Sometimes, you might want to create a table using data obtained from another table via SELECT. For illustration purposes, we will first create a test table:

```
CREATE TABLE TBL_CUSTOMER_TEST AS
SELECT *
FROM TBL_CUSTOMER;
```

This statement creates the table called TBL_CUSTOMER_TEST with the structure from the SQL query. In this case, we have selected all fields from the table TBL_CUSTOMER and TBL_CUSTOMER_TEST will therefore be structurally similar to TBL_CUSTOMER. In addition, the data provided in the SQL statement are added in the new table. We do not need to use COMMIT since this is a DDL command. This is a simple way to copy a table with its contents. If you are only interested in the structure but not the contents, you can add a condition such as WHERE 1=2. This can never be fulfilled for any data record and thus no data is copied.

Let us now delete the table and add the CUSTOMER_NO, FIRST_NAME, and SURNAME columns into the new table for all customers.

```
TRUNCATE TABLE TBL_CUSTOMER_TEST;

INSERT INTO TBL_CUSTOMER_TEST (CUSTOMER_NO, FIRST_NAME, SURNAME)
SELECT CUSTOMER_NO, FIRST_NAME, SURNAME
FROM TBL_CUSTOMERS;

COMMIT;
```

The INSERT INTO statement has the same structure as usual. The only difference is that instead of using the VALUES clause, we now have an SQL statement. Here, you can use arbitrarily complex SQL statements if they have the same structure (i.e. same number of fields and same data types).

Next, we are going to delete two customers and then re-add the two missing customers using a somewhat more complex SQL statement. We can do this using the following subquery:

```
DELETE TBL_CUSTOMER_TEST
WHERE CUSTOMER_NO IN(5,6,7);

COMMIT;

INSERT INTO TBL_CUSTOMER_TEST
SELECT *
FROM TBL_CUSTOMER customer_old
WHERE NOT EXISTS (
        SELECT 1
        FROM TBL_CUSTOMER_TEST customer_new
        WHERE customer_new.CUSTOMER_NO=customer_old.CUSTOMER_NO
```

```
);
COMMIT;
```

Using a simple SELECT *, we can now check if all datasets are once again available in the table. Here, you can identify the last datasets to be added as all their fields are filled. Here, all records from TBL_CUSTOMER are selected in the last SQL. Each of them is checked to see if the same customer number already exists in TBL_CUSTOMER_TEST. If it doesn't, the dataset is added. If the customer number already exists, the dataset is ignored. The result is then added to the table via INSERT INTO.

You can also complement the UPDATE statement with subqueries:

```
UPDATE TBL_CUSTOMER_TEST customer_new
SET GENDER=(
        SELECT UPPER(GENDER)
        FROM TBL_CUSTOMER customer_old
        WHERE customer_old.CUSTOMER_NO=customer_new.CUSTOMER_NO
);

COMMIT;
```

In this example, we have gone through all seven datasets in the new table TBL_CUSTOMER_TEST and used the subquery to select the corresponding dataset from TBL_CUSTOMER (using the customer number) and then returned the GENDER field. Here, all values have also been converted to uppercase letters. When using UPDATE, you must make sure that the subquery only returns one value. Otherwise, you get corresponding error messages.

You can also combine DELETE with subqueries. Below is an example. We will first create a copy of the product table and then delete it in the product table again:

```
CREATE TABLE TBL_PRODUCT_TEST AS
SELECT *
FROM TBL_PRODUCT;

DELETE TBL_PRODUCT
WHERE PRODUCT_NO NOT IN(
        SELECT PRODUCT_NO
        FROM TBL_ORDER_POS
);

COMMIT;
```

Here, we have used the IN operator and deleted all products that are not in TBL_ORDER_POS.

Exercise 7: To simplify future evaluations, we need a special table listing down the sales and commissions of each seller. The table should consist of four columns (EMPLOYEE_NO, MONTH, SALES, COMMISSION):
1. Create a corresponding table (TBL_COMM_SALES)
2. Use INSERT to first fill the fields EMPLOYEE_NO, MONTH, and SALES for all employees.
3. UPDATE the commission column

TOP-N queries

In practice, you often need to create a TOP-N report. For example, you might need a report with the top three selling products. So far, we have been able to calculate the sales per product as well as sort these in descending order. What is missing is a way to select the first three items, i.e. some kind of numbering.

To do this, we can use the ROWNUM pseudo-column. This gives you a row numbering from a table or subquery. Below is a simple example that sorts the customers by age and displays the 3 oldest customers:

```
SELECT *
FROM (
    SELECT CUSTOMER_NO, FIRST_NAME, SURNAME, DoB
    FROM TBL_CUSTOMERS
    ORDER BY 4 ASC
)
WHERE ROWNUM<=3
```

Result:

	CUSTOMER_NO	FIRSTNAME	SURNAME	DATE_OF_BIRTH
1	4	Hubertus	Meyer-Huber	15.07.58 00:00:00
2	5	Hanna	von Bergmann	17.09.65 00:00:00
3	7	Fabian	Lindemann	01.09.73 00:00:00

Exercises:

1) Create a list with all orders that are above the average sales of all orders. Proceed as follows:
   a) Calculate the average sales for all orders (not the order item)
   b) Use the result from a) to create the entire list

2) Create a list with the sales per day for the 1st quarter of 2013. In addition, display the daily sales share in the monthly sales. Use subqueries!

3) Calculate the sales share of each city in the total sales.

4) Which product group has not had any product orders? Use a subquery!

5) Which customers have had more sales than 66% of the sales of the customer with the highest sales?

6)
   a) Create a copy of the table TBL_PRODUCT without data. Next, add the products that are priced above the average price of all products.
   b) Add a column called AVG_PRICE_GROUP of the type NUMBER(10,2) in the table from (a) and fill it with the average price of the respective price group.

7) Create a list of the TOP 3 products.

8) Create a list of the drivers and add a column showing the number of orders delivered by each driver in April and May 2013. Also, calculate the variance between these two months.

9) Create a list of the cities with their respective flop product.

7 Set operations

Every SQL query usually returns a result set consisting of datasets. In each relational database, we have the so-called set operations with which you can create the standard sets already known from algebra (union, intersection, difference, etc.). This chapter will focus on these set operators.

UNION and UNION ALL

UNION returns all datasets from query 1 plus all datasets from query 2. Here, both queries (1 & 2). Otherwise, a corresponding error message is returned.

Figure 14: UNION ALL

UNION ALL returns a set consisting of the blue circle plus the green circle. If there are any duplicates, they are also included in the end result.

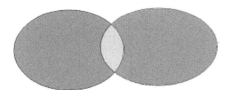

Figure 15: UNION

UNION returns a set consisting of the blue circle plus the green circle plus the orange circle. Any duplicates are eliminated and these datasets only appear once in the result set. These are represented by the orange section.

The example below should provide a clear illustration of the syntax:

```
SELECT CUSTOMER_NO, FIRST_NAME, SURNAME, 1 AS QUERY
FROM TBL_CUSTOMER
WHERE CITY='Hamburg'

UNION

SELECT CUSTOMER_NO, FIRST_NAME, SURNAME, 2 AS QUERY
```

```
FROM TBL_CUSTOMER
WHERE CITY<>'Hamburg'
```

Result:

	CUSTOMER_NO	FIRSTNAME	SURNAME	QUERY
1	1 Horst	Huber		1
2	2 Erika	Schmidt		1
3	3 Bert	Mueller		1
4	4 Hubertus	Meyer-Huber		2
5	5 Hanna	von Bergmann		2
6	6 Tobias	Maier		2
7	7 Fabian	Lindemann		2

In the above example, we have two simple queries. One of them returns the customer numbers, first names, and surnames of all customers from Hamburg. The second returns the details of all the other customers. We have also added an extra column with the value 1 for all datasets from the 1st query and 2 for those from the 2nd query. As you can see, the result set equals the datasets from the 1st query plus those from the 2nd query.

Using UNION creates this result set and removes any duplicates. In the example, both queries return disjoint sets (i.e. no dataset in the 1st query is in the 2nd and vice versa). Thus, no datasets are eliminated.

On the contrary, UNION ALL does not eliminate duplicates. Below is a second example to help illustrate the difference between UNION and UNION ALL:

```
SELECT CUSTOMER_NO, FIRST_NAME, SURNAME
FROM TBL_CUSTOMER
WHERE CUSTOMER_NO IN(1,2)

UNION

SELECT CUSTOMER_NO, FIRST_NAME, SURNAME
FROM TBL_CUSTOMER
WHERE CUSTOMER_NO IN(2,3)
```

Result:

	CUSTOMER_NO	FIRSTNAME	SURNAME
1	1 Horst	Huber	
2	2 Erika	Schmidt	
3	3 Bert	Mueller	

As we can see, customer number 2 is only listed once in the result set, although she appears in both subqueries. We had to remove the column with the query number for the UNION operator to function properly in our example. If we now use UNION ALL instead of UNION, we get the following result from our example above:

Result:

CUSTOMER_NO	FIRSTNAME	SURNAME
1	1 Horst	Huber
2	2 Erika	Schmidt
3	2 Erika	Schmidt
4	3 Bert	Mueller

Customer 2 now appears twice in the result set i.e., once from the 1st query and once from the 2nd.

Exercise 1: Create a list with the 2 best and 2 worst selling products. Mark them as TOP and FLOP respectively and display the number, name, and sales of each of the products.

INTERSECT

The INTERSECT operation returns the datasets that are true for both query 1 and query 2. This is illustrated by the figure below. Here, the intersection is represented by the yellow area:

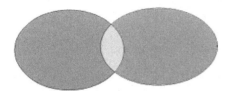

Figure 16: INTERSECTION

INTERSECT has the same structure as UNION – it needs to be similar. If we take our last query in the UNION section and replace UNION ALL with INTERSECT, we get:

```
SELECT CUSTOMER_NO, FIRST_NAME, SURNAME
FROM TBL_CUSTOMER
WHERE CUSTOMER_NO IN(1,2)

INTERSECT

SELECT CUSTOMER_NO, FIRST_NAME, SURNAME
FROM TBL_CUSTOMER
WHERE CUSTOMER_NO IN(2,3)
```

Result:

CUSTOMER_NO	FIRSTNAME	SURNAME
1	2 Erika	Schmidt

This returns customer no. 2 since she appears in both subqueries. Customers 1 and 3 only appear once in one of the two queries and are therefore not in the intersection of the two result sets.

Exercise 2: Which products (no., name) were purchased by both male and female customers? Use set operations!

Difference (MINUS)

The MINUS operator can be used to determine differences in the two query results quite easily.

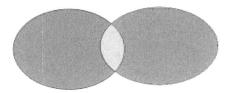

Figure 17: Difference (MINUS)

Let us assume that we are interested in the blue query MINUS the green query. Our result would be the blue area. The orange part and the green areas are hereby excluded.

Below is an example:

```
SELECT CUSTOMER_NO, FIRST_NAME, SURNAME
FROM TBL_CUSTOMER
WHERE CUSTOMER_NO IN(1,2)

MINUS

SELECT CUSTOMER_NO, FIRST_NAME, SURNAME
FROM TBL_CUSTOMER
WHERE CUSTOMER_NO IN(2,3)
```

Result:

CUSTOMER_NO	FIRSTNAME	SURNAME
1	1 Horst	Huber

This takes the result set from the 1st query and subtracts that of the second query. Customer no. 2 is now excluded since she appears in both sets. Customer no. 3 is not in the first set and is therefore not included.

Exercise 3: Use set operations to generate a list of products (no. + name) that have never been sold.

Exercises

1) Display the best-selling product in Hamburg and best-selling product in Kiel using a query. Make sure to also include the respective sales.

2) Which of the two cities ranks higher in terms of the number of orders and total sales?

3) Add the missing products in the table TBL_PRODUCT_TEST (created in chapter 7). Fill the AVG_PRICE_GROUP column with zeroes. Use appropriate set operators!

4) Create a list showing the sales per product, per product group, and the total sales. You should first display the sales of the products in the 1st group, then the sales for product group 1, then the sales for the products of the 2nd group, the total sales of product group 2, and so on. The last row should be the total sales.

8   Creating (DDL) and filling (DML) tables

In this chapter, we will learn how you can use DDL to create and delete tables as well as modify the structure. We will also use DML to fill tables with data as well as delete and modify data.

Creating and deleting tables

To create tables, we use the CREATE TABLE statement. For example, you can generate the structure for TBL_CUSTOMER using the following statement:

```
CREATE TABLE TBL_CUSTOMER(
        CUSTOMER_NO   NUMBER(10,0) NOT NULL,
        FIRST_NAME   VARCHAR2(25) NOT NULL,
        SURNAME   VARCHAR2(25) NOT NULL,
        STREET VARCHAR2(50),
        ZIP_Code   VARCHAR2(5),
        CITY   VARCHAR2(20),
        GENDER VARCHAR2(1) CHECK (GENDER IN('M', 'F', 'm', 'f')),
        DoB DATE DEFAULT TO_DATE('01.01.1900' ,'DD.MM.YYYY')
);
```

This lists down all columns separated by commas. Every column must have at least a name and data type. Oracle offers diverse data types. You can find a comprehensive list at:

   http://docs.oracle.com/cd/B28359_01/server.111/b28286/sql_elements001.htm#SQLRF50951

We will use the data types listed below for our examples in this book. These are also the most commonly used data types:

*   **NUMBER ([total no. of digits][, decimal places])** for numbers
*   **VARCHAR2 (Max. no. of characters)** for text
*   **DATE** for date/time

You can specify the total no. of digits and the decimal places in NUMBER columns, but it is not mandatory. However, you must specify the maximum number of characters for VARCHAR2 fields.

You can define standard values using **DEFAULT** for every column. In our example, we have done this for the date of birth. If, for example, the date of birth is not entered when adding new datasets, the specified standard value is used.

Similarly, you can also specify the so-called **CHECK constraints** for each column. These check the data for specific conditions. If the conditions are not fulfilled, the respective dataset cannot be added or edited. For example, we have used the **NOT NULL** constraint for the columns CUSTOMER_NO, FIRST_NAME, and SURNAME. Thus, these fields must be filled with data when adding or modifying the datasets. The fields in the other columns can be left empty. In the gender column, we have a **CHECK (condition)**. This makes sure that only values M, F, m, f can be added in this column.

Conditions can be any expression, just like when using the WHERE condition in an SQL statement. This is described in more detail in the 4th chapter.

Assuming we have made an error and would like to rename the table we just created, we use the following statement:

```
RENAME TBL_CUSTOMERS TO TBL_CUSTOMERS2;
```

To delete the table that we have just created, we need the following statement:

```
DROP TABLE TBL_CUSTOMERS2;
```

Exercise 1: Create the table TBL_EMPLOYEES as per the data model, but without primary keys and foreign keys.

Creating foreign key relationships using constraints

Chapter 1 described relationships between tables as well as the referential integrity, which can be ensured in the database using foreign key constraints. In this section, we will enhance our data model using corresponding constraints. We will use tables TBL_PRODUCT and TBL_PRODUCT_GROUP as examples. According to the data model (chapter 2), the two tables are related via the PRODUCT_GROUP_NO column.

To be able to add foreign key constraints, the referenced table must have a defined primary key. In addition, the table must already be existent. The following statement first creates the table TBL_PRODUCT_GROUP with the corresponding PRIMARY KEY:

```
CREATE TABLE TBL_PRODUCT_GROUP(
        PRODUCT_GROUP_NO  NUMBER(5,0) NOT NULL,
        NAME  VARCHAR2(25),
        CONSTRAINT PK_PROD_GROUP PRIMARY KEY (PRODUCT_GROUP_NO)
);
```

Since every product group must have a number for it to be referenced by the products, we have defined a CHECK NOT NULL constraint. The primary key is then created using the **CONSTRAINT ....
PRIMARY KEY** clause. The constraint requires a name, in our case PK_PROD_GROUP. With the primary key, it is automatically checked if every row has a unique value in the PRODUCT_GROUP_NO column. This is important to ensure that the product table has a unique link to the PRODUCT_GROUP. The DBMS now checks every new product group to ensure that it has a unique number. If it doesn't, it returns a corresponding error message.

We can now create the table TBL_PRODUCT, define the foreign key, and then add a reference to the table TBL_PRODUCT_GROUP:

```
CREATE TABLE TBL_PRODUCT(
        PRODUCT_NO  NUMBER(5, 0) NOT NULL,
        NAME  VARCHAR2(25),
        PRICE  NUMBER(10,2),
        PRODUCT_GROUP_NO  NUMBER(5, 0) NOT NULL,
        CONSTRAINT PK_PRODUCT PRIMARY KEY (PRODUCT_NO),
        CONSTRAINT FK_PROD_PROD_GROUP FOREIGN KEY (PRODUCT_GROUP_NO)
        REFERENCES TBL_PRODUCT_GROUP(PRODUCT_GROUP_NO)
);
```

In this table as well, we have already defined the primary key, CHECK NOT NULL constraints on the PRODUCT_NO and PRODUCT_GROUP_NO columns. The foreign key is defined using the CONTRAINT ... FOREIGN KEY statement. REFERENCES is then used to establish a link to the table TBL_PRODUCT_GROUP.

Next, we will try to add the following dataset to check whether the foreign key relation is working:

```
INSERT INTO TBL_PRODUCT VALUES(1, 'Rump steak', 20.95, 1);
COMMIT;
```

This returns the following error message:

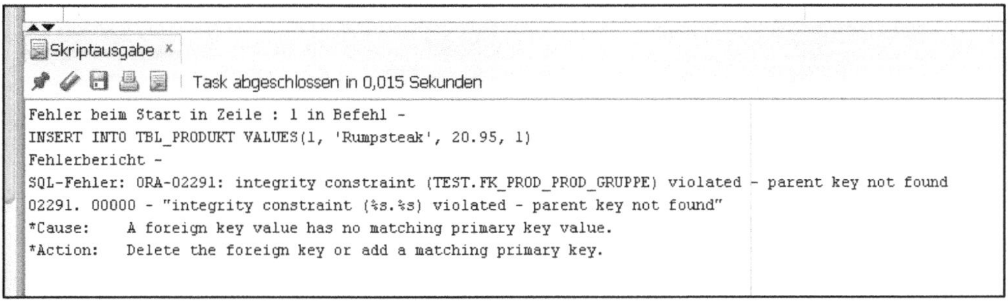

Figure 10: Error message due to violated FK constraint

The problem is that there is still no dataset in the product group. Thus, the referential integrity cannot be ensured and the dataset is rejected. We could modify the above example and start by first creating a corresponding product group and then try to add 'Rump steak' in the product table:

```
INSERT INTO TBL_PRODUCT_GROUP VALUES(1, 'Meat dishes');
COMMIT;

INSERT INTO TBL_PRODUCT VALUES(1, 'Rump steak', 20.95, 1);
COMMIT;
```

This works quite well and we get the message that the new dataset has been added successfully.

Sometimes, it is easier to deactivate the constraints for a short time if you want to perform extensive data manipulation. You can then reactivate the constraints afterwards. Your new datasets will then be checked to see if they meet the condition of the constraints. However, this can result in problems that might be very difficult to solve. To deactivate a constraint, use the following syntax:

```
ALTER TABLE TBL_PRODUCT DISABLE CONSTRAINT FK_PROD_PROD_GROUP;
```

To reactivate the constraint, use the following syntax:

```
ALTER TABLE TBL_PRODUCT ENABLE CONSTRAINT FK_PROD_PROD_GROUP;
```

Exercise 2: Create the table TBL_ORDER as per the data model, including the primary key and add the foreign key constraint to the table TBL_CUSTOMER. Here, first delete TBL_CUSTOMER and then re-create the table including the primary key.

Changing the table structure afterwards

You can also change the table structure later. This means that you can add, delete, or modify columns and constraints later. This is generally done using the ALTER TABLE statement with different options:

ALTER TABLE option	Description
ADD CONSTRAINT ... PRIMARY KEY (...)	Adds a PRIMARY KEY constraint to the table
ADD CONSTRAINT ... FOREIGN KEY (...) REFERENCES ...	Adds a FOREIGN KEY constraint to the table
ADD CONSTRAINT CHECK ...	Adds a CHECK constraint to the table
ADD (col1def, col2def, ...)	Adds one or more columns to the table. Col1def, col2def corresponds to the syntax of the 'Defs' column in the CREATE TABLE statement.
MODIFY (col1def, col2def, ...)	Changes one or more columns in the table. Col1def, col2def corresponds to the syntax of the 'Defs' column in the CREATE TABLE statement.
DROP (col1name, col2name, ...)	Deletes the columns with the names col1name, col2name, ... from the table.
DROP CONSTRAINT const_name	Removes the constraint const_name from the table

Table 1: ALTER TABLE options

For example, if we want to add a column to the TBL_CUSTOMER table, we would use the following statement:

```
ALTER TABLE TBL_CUSTOMER ADD (TEST VARCHAR2(10) DEFAULT 'n/a' NOT NULL);
```

If we now noticed that the column should be of NUMBER type, we can alter it as follows using MODIFY:

```
ALTER TABLE TBL_CUSTOMER MODIFY (TEST NUMBER DEFAULT -1);
```

Changing columns afterwards can be problematic at times, especially if the table has already been filled with data. If you want to keep these data and at the same time need to modify the data type of a specific column, you can start by first adding the column and then use update to copy the values from the old column while performing any necessary transformations at the same time. Once done, you can then delete the old column.

You can do this for all the other modification options, i.e. using the basic syntax ALTER TABLE <tab_name> <ALTER option>.

Exercise 3: First, delete the TEST column from the table TBL_CUSTOMER and then add a CREATED_ON column. This new column should contain the date on which the respective dataset was added in the table. Here, the date should be inserted automatically without you having to enter it manually, i.e. using the 'sysdate' function.

Exercise 4: Add a primary key in the table TBL_EMPLOYEES and a foreign key in TBL_ORDER (sellers).

Adding datasets

Once we have created the data structures, we can then proceed to add corresponding data into the tables. We had already looked at two simple INSERT INTO statements when learning about the foreign key constraints. The example below should help illustrate the more detailed syntax:

INSERT INTO TBL_CUSTOMER
VALUES (1, 'Horst', 'Huber', 'Karolinenweg 11a', '20357', 'Hamburg', 'M', *to_date*('01.05.1947', 'DD.MM.YYYY'), **null**);

COMMIT;

The above statement has been used to add a dataset to the table TBL_CUSTOMER. The second *COMMIT* command physically inserts the data. If you were to omit the COMMIT statement, other users would not be able to see this dataset in the table. The inserted values are entered after "Values (" and must be in the same order as the columns in the table. All columns must be filled with values. If you want to use a different order or only wish to fill certain columns, you can do this by specifying the respective columns after the name of the table. Below is an example:

INSERT INTO TBL_CUSTOMER (CUSTOMER_NO, FIRST_NAME, SURNAME)
VALUES (2, 'Erika', 'Schmidt');

INSERT INTO TBL_CUSTOMER (CUSTOMER_NO, FIRST_NAME, SURNAME)
VALUES (3, 'Bert', 'Müller');

COMMIT;

This adds two datasets. However, only the specified columns are filled (NOT NULL constraint) and the two datasets saved simultaneously.

Result:

CUSTOMER_NO	FIRSTNAME	SURNAME	STREET	ZIP_CODE	CITY	GENDER	DATE_OF_BIRTH	CREATION_DATE
1	3 Bert	Mueller	(null)	(null)	(null)	(null)	01.01.00 00:00:00	18.08.17 11:37:54
2	1 Horst	Huber	Karolinenweg 11a	20357	Hamburg	M	01.05.47 00:00:00	(null)
3	2 Erika	Schmidt	(null)	(null)	(null)	(null)	01.01.00 00:00:00	18.08.17 11:37:54

As we can see from the above result, we have three datasets in the table. In the first one, we added data in all columns—except for the creation date which is <null> (since we were required to enter something else). As for the other two datasets, we only filled the CUSTOMER_NO, FIRST_NAME, and SURNAME fields. All the other fields are <null>—except for the creation date. Although we did not enter any data into this field, but we had defined the column such that the system date should be inserted if no data is entered. Thus, we have the date on which the dataset was added (i.e. on 16.06.2014 in the above example).

Editing datasets

The UPDATE statement is used to edit datasets. Let us look at the following example where we add the columns STREET, ZIP_Code, and CITY for the customers with customer numbers 2 and 3:

```
UPDATE TBL_CUSTOMER
SET STREET='Goethestrasse 5', ZIP_Code='22512', CITY='Hamburg'
WHERE CUSTOMER_NO=2;

UPDATE TBL_CUSTOMER
SET STREET='Schwedenweg 22', ZIP_Code='22123', CITY='Hamburg'
WHERE CUSTOMER_NO=3;

COMMIT;
```

The columns to be edited are assigned the new values after the SET command. Here, you can also enter calculations or other columns. The WHERE clause enables you to define where you want to update the respective datasets. The WHERE clause is described in more detail in chapter 4. Here is another example of an UPDATE statement:

```
ALTER TABLE TBL_PRODUCT ADD (PRICE_NEW NUMBER);

UPDATE TBL_PRODUCT
SET PRICE_NEW=PRICE*5;

COMMIT;

SELECT *
FROM TBL_PRODUCT;
```

Result:

	PRODUCT_NO	NAME	PRICE	PRODUCT_GROUP_NO	PRICE_NEW
1	1	Rumpsteak	20,95	1	104,75
2	2	Grill platter	14,95	1	74,75
3	3	Pizza Salami	5,6	2	28
4	4	Pizza Hawai	6,1	2	30,5
5	5	Pizza Thunfisch	6,1	2	30,5
6	6	Pizza Spezial	6,95	2	34,75
7	7	Pizza Vital	5,8	2	29
8	8	Spagetti Bolognese	4,5	3	22,5
9	9	Lasagne	4,5	3	22,5
10	10	Tagliatelle Carbonara	4,5	3	22,5

We have first added a new column. The column is initially empty. We then update it using the UPDATE statement and calculate PRICE_NEW by multiplying the value in the PRICE column by 5. This is performed for every dataset in the product table since no restriction was specified using the WHERE clause.

Deleting datasets

There are two ways of deleting datasets. The first is by using the DELETE statement:

```
DELETE TBL_CUSTOMER
WHERE CUSTOMER_NO=2;


COMMIT;


SELECT *
FROM TBL_CUSTOMER
```

Result:

CUSTOMER_NO	FIRSTNAME	SURNAME	STREET	ZIP_CODE	CITY	GENDER	DATE_OF_BIRTH	CREATION_DATE
1	3 Bert	Mueller	(null)	(null)	(null)	(null)	01.01.00 00:00:00	18.08.17 11:37:54
2	1 Horst	Huber	Karolinenweg 11a	20357	Hamburg	M	01.05.47 00:00:00	(null)

The statement deletes the datasets with the specified customer number. In our example, this corresponds to exactly one dataset. If you were to omit the WHERE clause, the statement would delete all the datasets in the table. You must use COMMIT to save changes when using DELETE as well. If you later notice that you made an error during the deletion (e.g., in the WHERE clause), you can go back to the original status using ROLLBACK. However, ROLLBACK only works if you have not yet used COMMIT.

Another way of deleting data from a table is using the TRUNCATE TABLE command:

```
ALTER TABLE TBL_ORDER DISABLE CONSTRAINT FK _ORDER_CUSTOMER;


TRUNCATE TABLE TBL_CUSTOMER;


ALTER TABLE TBL_ORDER ENABLE CONSTRAINT FK _ORDER_CUSTOMER;


SELECT *
FROM TBL_CUSTOMER;
```

When using truncate, you must make sure that the constraints are deactivated. Truncate is not a DML action and therefore does not run within a transaction. This is why you should not use this command if the constraints are activated.

Result:

The query does not return any data.

What do you notice? COMMIT is missing. This is because, strictly speaking, TRUNCATE TABLE is not a DML command (data manipulating language) but rather a DDL command (e.g., CREATE TABLE). This command therefore does not run within a transaction. For large amounts of data, this is very advantageous in terms of the runtime for deleting an entire table. However, no ROLLBACK can be performed for TRUNCATE TABLE commands. The data are deleted immediately and permanently.

Exercises

1) Add one dataset to the table TBL_CUSTOMER:
   - Customer no.: 1
   - FIRST_NAME: Hugo
   - SURNAME: Schmidt

2)
   - Create the table TBL_ORDER_POS according to the data model, including a primary and foreign key constraint referencing to the table TBL_ORDER
   - Next, add one dataset to the tables TBL_ORDER_POS and TBL_ORDER:
     - TBL_ORDER_POS: (Order:1, product:25, number:1)
     - TBL_ORDER: (Order:1, date: 01.01.2014, picked up:0, customer:1, driver:1, employee:1)

3) Create a foreign key between TBL_PRODUCT and TBL_ORDER_POS. This will probably return an error. What is the cause of this error? Change the <u>data</u> to eliminate this error.

4) Clear the tables TBL_ORDER_POS and TBL_ORDER using the DELETE statement. What do you need to look out for?

5) Look at the INSERT statements in the TBL_CUSTOMER_INSERT.SQL file. How should you change the structure of the TBL_CUSTOMER table for you to be able to add the data using the INSERT statements without an error?

6) The following files are available in the course directory. They contain INSERT statements that are used to fill the respective table with data:
   - TBL_ORDER_INSERT.SQL
   - TBL_ORDER_POS_INSERT.SQL
   - TBL_CUSTOMER_INSERT.SQL
   - TBL_EMPLOYEE_INSERT.SQL
   - TBL_PRODUCT.SQL
   - TBL_PRODUCT_GROUP.SQL

   What must you look out for before running these scripts?

9   Miscellaneous

Classic views

Next, we will look at the concept of views. A view can basically be described as an SQL statement saved under a name in the database. It can be used in other SQLs just like a normal table. In the example below, we will first create a simple view showing us the customers from Hamburg and then access this result using another SQL:

```
CREATE VIEW V_CUSTOMERS_HAMBURG AS
SELECT *
FROM TBL_CUSTOMER
WHERE CITY='Hamburg';


SELECT CUSTOMER_NO, FIRST_NAME, SURNAME, ZIP_Code, CITY
FROM V_CUSTOMERS_HAMBURG;
```

Result:

CUSTOMER_NO	FIRSTNAME	SURNAME	ZIP_CODE	CITY
1	1 Horst	Huber	20357	Hamburg
2	2 Erika	Schmidt	22512	Hamburg
3	3 Bert	Mueller	22123	Hamburg

You can use views just like you can use tables. You can also update views, but only if they are related to a certain table. The following example uses the view created above and links it with the order data. The result is saved in a new view:

```
CREATE VIEW V_NO_OF_ORDERS_CUSTOMERS_HH AS
SELECT  k.CUSTOMER_NO, k.FIRST_NAME, k.SURNAME,
        Count(distinct b.ORDER_NO) AS NO_OF_ORDERS
FROM V_CUSTOMER_HAMBURG k
   JOIN TBL_ORDER b ON k.CUSTOMER_NO=b.CUSTOMER_NO
GROUP BY k.CUSTOMER_NO, k.FIRST_NAME, k.SURNAME;


SELECT *
FROM V_NO_OF_ORDERS_CUSTOMERS_HH;
```

Result:

CUSTOMER_NO	FIRSTNAME	SURNAME	ANZ_ORDERS
1	3 Bert	Mueller	37
2	1 Horst	Huber	39
3	2 Erika	Schmidt	32

To delete a view, use the following syntax:

```
DROP VIEW V_NO_OF_ORDERS_CUSTOMERS_HH;
```

Since views are only a saved SQL and therefore do not contain any data, the results are always up to date. This means that if we use the view V_NO_OF_ORDERS_CUSTOMERS_HH on two different days, the contents can be totally different – depending on whether new orders were added in the underlying table during the period in between.

Clearly, this offers the great advantage of e.g. being able to store certain, recurring queries as views in the database and then access them easily using, for example, Excel or have other colleagues access them.

Exercise 1: Create a new view named V_SALES_PRODUCT, which returns the total sales per product. All product's columns should hereby be output.

Permissions in Oracle

Oracle has diverse options with which you can manage and control access writes to objects, thus enabling you to exactly specify who is allowed to access which object. Here, there are two commands, **GRANT** and **REVOKE**, which you can use to grant and revoke access rights. The owner of an object, i.e. the DB administrator or person who created the object, can therefore specify specific rights. In the following example, we will assign the users named TEST2 and TEST3 read access rights to the table TBL_CUSTOMERS. This requires us to be logged in as TEST (owner of TBL_CUSTOMER). You can also simply specify a certain user, or use the keyword **PUBLIC** to grant access to all users:

```
GRANT SELECT ON TBL_CUSTOMER TO TEST2, TEST3;
```

We can now log in as the user TEST2 or TEST3 and check the tables that we can access. We can do this either by going to the SQL developer and navigating to Other user -> TEST -> Tables in the object browser (left-hand side) or by trying out the following SQL:

```
SELECT *
FROM TEST.TBL_CUSTOMER;
```

Result:

	CUSTOMER_NO	FIRSTNAME	SURNAME	STREET	ZIP_CODE	CITY	GENDER	DATE_OF_BIRTH
1	1	Horst	Huber	Karolinenweg 11a	20357	Hamburg	M	01.05.75 00:00:00
2	2	Erika	Schmidt	Goethestraße 5	22512	Hamburg	F	05.10.85 00:00:00
3	3	Bert	Mueller	Schwedenweg 22	22123	Hamburg	m	03.02.79 00:00:00
4	4	Hubertus	Meyer-Huber	Hamburger Strasse 67	24106	Kiel	M	15.07.58 00:00:00
5	5	Hanna	von Bergmann	Werftstrasse 22	24145	Kiel	f	17.09.65 00:00:00
6	6	Tobias	Maier	Foerdeweg 2	26105	Flensburg	M	03.03.92 00:00:00
7	7	Fabian	Lindemann	Kieler Strasse 102	23809	Luebeck	m	01.09.73 00:00:00

As we can see, we have access to all the data in TBL_CUSTOMER. Please note that you must write the name of the other users or schema for Oracle to address the correct table.

Rights are revoked in a similar manner:

```
REVOKE SELECT ON TBL_CUSTOMER FROM TEST2;
```

The table below lists down all possible access rights:

Privilege	Description

SELECT	Read access. Columns cannot be specified.
UPDATE <column1, column2, ...>	Changing access. You can specify the columns that can be accessed. Grants access to all columns if no column is specified
DELETE	Deleting datasets
INSERT	Adding new datasets
REFERENCE <column1, column2, ...>	Creating foreign keys. You can specify the columns that can be accessed. Grants access to all columns if no column is specified.
ALL PRIVILEGES	All access rights to the table

Table 6: Overview of access rights

These rights are specifically intended for tables and views. There are other rights for other objects such as procedures and so on, but we will not cover them in this course. Creation of users and assignment of roles will also not be covered in this course since this is primarily a task for database administrators.

Exercise 2: Write a construct that grants user TEST2 access to only the columns CUSTOMER_NO, FIRST_NAME, and SURNAME in the table TBL_CUSTOMERS?

Additional useful functions

This section will introduce a few more useful functions. We will first start by learning how to use IF THEN ELSE constructs in calculations e.g., to categorize products in three groups based on their sales. Here, you can use the following command:

```
CASE
        WHEN <CONDITION1> THEN <EXPRESSION1>
        WHEN <CONDITION2> THEN <EXPRESSON2>
        ....
        ELSE <EXPRESSION>
END
```

Here is a simple example:

```
SELECT PRODUCT_NO, NAME, SALES,
    CASE
        WHEN SALES<700 THEN 'A'
        WHEN SALES BETWEEN 700 AND 1000 THEN 'B'
        ELSE 'C'
    END AS SALES_GROUP
FROM V_SALES_PRODUCT
ORDER BY 3 ASC
```

Result:

	PRODUCT_NO	NAME	TURNOVER	TURNOVER_GROUP
1	11	Coke 0,331	348,25	A
2	13	Water 1,51 with gas	428	A
3	12	Beer Holsten 0,51	532	A
4	14	Fruit salad	696	A
5	15	Tiramisu	832	B
6	9	Lasagne	873	B
7	8	Spagetti Bolognese	873	B
8	10	Tagliatelle Carbonara	1062	C
9	3	Pizza Salami	1181,6	C
10	5	Pizza Thunfisch	1195,6	C
11	4	ᴘᵢᵤᵤ ᵤᵤᵤᵢ	1250,5	C

Next, we will look at the **DECODE** function. This enables you to perform IF comparisons relatively easily – for example, if you wanted to extend the above example to specify the sales bandwidth for the respective groups. You can have multiple arguments in this function:

DECODE (<column>, <value1>, <replacement value1>, <value2>, ..., <other value>)

In our example, this would look like this:

```
SELECT x.*,
    DECODE(SALES_GROUP, 'A', '€0 ... €700', 'B', '>€700 ... €1000', '>€100 ... ')
    AS GROUP_NAME
FROM (
  SELECT PRODUCT_NO, NAME, SALES,
        CASE
            WHEN SALES<700 THEN 'A'
            WHEN SALES BETWEEN 700 AND 1000 THEN 'B'
            ELSE 'C'
        END AS SALES_GROUP
    FROM V_SALES_PRODUCT
    ORDER BY 3 ASC
) x
```

Result:

	PRODUCT_NO	NAME	TURNOVER	TURNOVER_GROUP	GROUP_BEZ
1	11	Coke 0,331	348,25	A	0€ ... 700€
2	13	Water 1,51 with gas	428	A	0€ ... 700€
3	12	Beer Holsten 0,51	532	A	0€ ... 700€
4	14	Fruit salad	696	A	0€ ... 700€
5	15	Tiramisu	832	B	>700€ ... 1000€
6	9	Lasagne	873	B	>700€ ... 1000€
7	8	Spagetti Bolognese	873	B	>700€ ... 1000€
8	10	Tagliatelle Carbonara	1062	C	>1000€ ...
9	3	Pizza Salami	1181,6	C	>1000€ ...
10	5	Pizza Thunfisch	1195,6	C	>1000€ ...
11	4	ᴘᵢᵤᵤ ᵤᵤᵤᵢ	1250,5	C	>1000€

The subquery is identical to the query in the CASE WHEN END example. The DECODE function now sits on top and checks the SALES_GROUP column from the subquery. If it has the value 'A', the function returns '€0 ... €700'. If the column has the value 'B', the function returns '>€700 ... €1000', etc.

Exercise 3: Create a view that checks all customers (customer no.) and displays per customer whether the customer has placed more than 5 orders or not.

Overview and introduction of analytical functions

Next, we will take a brief look at analytical functions. In chapter 6, we learned about groupings and aggregations. However, these are quite rigid and sometimes complex and cumbersome, e.g., if you wanted to combine a product sum and the total sum in a query. This is only possible via subqueries and a corresponding link.

Analytical functions now make it possible to create different calculations via different groupings and display them in a query. We will illustrate this using a simple example. Let us assume that we want to display the product groups with their respective sales and share in the total turnover:

```
SELECT DISTINCT
    grp.PRODUCT_GROUP_NO AS GROUP_NO,
    grp.NAME,

    SUM(sal.SALES) OVER() AS TOTAL_SALES,

    SUM(sal.SALES) OVER( PARTITION BY grp.PRODUCT_GROUP_NO) AS TOTAL_SALES

    round( SUM(sal.SALES) OVER( PARTITION BY grp.PRODUCT_GROUP_NO)
    / SUM(sal.SALES) OVER(),2) AS SHARE

FROM V_SALES_PRODUCT ums
    JOIN TBL_PRODUCT_GROUP grp ON sal.PRODUCT_GROUP_NO=grp.PRODUCT_GROUP_NO
ORDER BY 1
```

Result:

	PRODUCT_GROUP_NO	NAME	TURNOVER_GESAMT	TURNOVER_GROUP	ANTEIL
1	1	Meat dishes	20097,45	7850,1	0,39
2	2	Pizzas	20097,45	6603,1	0,33
3	3	Pasta	20097,45	2808	0,14
4	4	Drinks	20097,45	1308,25	0,07
5	5	Desserts	20097,45	1528	0,08

If you look at the calculation of the SALES_GROUP column, you notice right away the typical structure of an analytical calculation:

Function(<column>) OVER(PARTITION BY <column 1>, <column 2>, ...)

In our example, we have used the SUM function. You can also use other functions (e.g., AVG, MIN, MAX, count, count (distinct), etc.). <column> should be the column to be evaluated by the function. *OVER* (...) generally specifies the grouping level. If you leave it empty, the function is executed for all the evaluation data. You can see this in the calculation of the TOTAL_SALES column. Here, it has been left empty to calculate the total sum. If we wanted to specify groupings, we could do this using **PARTITION BY** and 1 to n columns. In this case, the function would be executed on each of these groups and assigned to the corresponding group. For example, we have calculated the sum per product group, i.e. we have specified the PRODUCT_GROUP_NO as the column in PARTITION BY. You can also use these calculations to generate more structuring calculations. This has been done in the SHARE column. Here, the two previous calculations have been reused to calculate the respective sales share.

Exercise 4: Create an evaluation that calculates the product sales and product group sales for every product. Sort your results by the product number. Do not use the V_SALES_PRODUCT view.

Another application example would be to calculate a cumulated sum, i.e. an evaluation showing the monthly sales as well as the cumulative sales from January to the current month. To do this, the analytical calculation would have to be extended using additional components:

```
SELECT DISTINCT
  x.*,
  SUM(SALES) OVER(
    ORDER BY MONTH ASC
    ROWS BETWEEN UNBOUNDED PRECEDING AND CURRENT ROW
  ) AS SALES_CUM
FROM (
  SELECT DISTINCT
    to_char(b.ORDER_DATE,'MM/YYYY') AS MONTH,
    SUM(bp.COUNT*p.PRICE) OVER(
      PARTITION BY to_char(b.ORDER_DATE,'MM/YYYY')
    ) AS SALES
  FROM TBL_ORDER b
  JOIN TBL_ORDER_POS bp ON b.ORDER_NO=bp.ORDER_NO
  JOIN TBL_PRODUCT p ON bp.PRODUCT_NO=p.PRODUCT_NO
  WHERE to_char(b.ORDER_DATE,'YYYY')='2013'
) x
ORDER BY 1
```

Result:

	MONTH	SALES	SALES_CUM
1	01/2013	2126,05	2126,05
2	02/2013	1381,35	3507,4
3	03/2013	1921,2	5428,6
4	04/2013	1804,1	7232,7
5	05/2013	1057,35	8290,05
6	06/2013	1259,85	9549,9
7	07/2013	1223,1	10773
8	08/2013	2049,7	12822,7

Looking at the result shows us that the cumulation works quite well. In the subquery, we have first used an analytical function to calculate the monthly sales. This was done for the year 2013. In the next query, we have then used another analytical function that goes through all the data from 2013.

ROWS BETWEEN UNBOUNDED PRECEDING AND CURRENT ROW is used to define a so-called window. In our case, this window has been applied dynamically, i.e. always runs from the 1st dataset of the partition to the current dataset. The general syntax is:

ROWS BETWEEN <limit 1> AND <limit 2>

with <limit>= <expression> PRECEDING | FOLLOWING or CURRENT ROW
with <expression>= UNBOUNDED or a numerical expression

UNBOUNDED is hereby used to specify that the window should run up to the start/end of the partition. **PRECEDING** refers to datasets before the current dataset whereas **FOLLOWING** refers to those after the current dataset. **CURRENT ROW** refers to the current dataset. This therefore enables you to define any window.

Due to the way the window function works, we must first create a subquery. If we fail to do this, the query granularity would no longer be at a monthly level since the data in the table is at a daily level and the analytical function would therefore be performed for every dataset. To this extent, we first calculate the first monthly sums and then use this result as a basis for a second analytical function.

In certain calculations, the order in which the datasets are added to the calculation also plays a role. You can sort the datasets using **ORDER BY**. This is important when calculating cumulative sums since the datasets must be sorted chronologically for the sums to be correct.

This is why we sorted the cumulative total by the MONTH in our calculation. When calculating the monthly sales in the subquery, the order does not matter since we are simply summing up all the datasets in a group.

Exercise 5: Create an evaluation that, instead of calculating the cumulative sum, displays the value of the previous month if existent (i.e. not possible for January).

The following functions are hereby available:

Function	Description
SUM, AVG, MAX, MIN, COUNT, COUNT(distinct)	Standard aggregate functions. Can be specified with and without a window as well as with and without sorting.
FIRST_VALUE (<column>) LAST_VALUE(<column>)	Returns the first/last dataset in a partition after sorting.
ROW_NUMBER()	Returns a numbering of the datasets within a partition.
RANK() DENSE_RANK()	Returns a ranking based on the sorting within a partition. In the case of RANK, a corresponding number of positions is left out if there are several datasets that have the same value. Example: If there are two first places, there wouldn't be a second with RANK. For DENSE_RANK, we will

	have two first places and then a second, third, etc. Always requires sorting.

Table 7: Overview of important analytical functions

There are many other functions and extensions of analytical functions. These will be presented and explained in detail in the second part of my SQL training series.

Exercises

(1) You have been tasked with reordering the rights for all tables of the user called TEST. To do this, first log in as user TEST and:
   (a) revoke all access rights that had been granted for the table TBL_CUSTOMER,
   (b) grant user TEST2 read access to the table TBL_PRODUCT,
   (c) grant the user TEST2 the right to edit the PRICE column in the table TBL_PRODUCT,
   (d) test the access rights granted above by logging in as TEST2 and accessing tables TBL_CUSTOMER and TBL_PRODUCT. Try to change the price of the product number 16 to 1.

(2)
   (a) Create a view that calculates the total sales based on the previously created V_PRODUCT_SALES view
   (b) Next, add a SALES_PRODUCT (NUMBER(10,2)) column to the table TBL_PRODUCT and fill it using the V_PRODUCT_SALES view
   (c) Add another column, SALES_SHARE (NUMBER(10,2)) and fill it using the view created above and the SALES_PRODUCT column added above. (Round them to 2 decimal places.)

(3) Create an evaluation that displays the best-performing product in every product group, once based on its sales and again based on the number of orders. Use the FIRST_VALUE function.

(4) Create a list showing the product groups with their products. Make sure to include the product sales as well as a ranking within the product group and a second ranking for all products. Include an extra column where you mark the best product in every product group with an '*'.

Have you enjoyed reading this book?

If you found this book useful,
I would really appreciate a short review.

Reviews help other people find this book.

Thank you and happy SQL coding!

About the author

I am working as a freelancing database developer, trainer and author. I am living in Kiel, Germany. For more than 10 years I am already working in this area. My customers are companies of different sizes from different industries (banking, engineering, medical, etc.).

Besides my regular work I am writing books and articles for my blog on database topics like SQL, NoSQL, MDX, Cognos, datawarehousing, etc. True to my motto „practical experiences for practical applications" a lot of practical tutorials and guidebooks are created in that process in order to help you finding your way through the database jungle.

More information about me: born in 1981, MSc in information management, experiences as customer and consultant.

Do you have further questions?

Just contact me via eMail: fabian@gaussling.com

Or get connected with me on…

    … XING

    … LinkedIn

    … Google+

    … Twitter

If you want more database knowledge, you can find it ….

    … on my BLOG: http://bi-solutions.gaussling.com

    … in my online database training: http://online-trainings.gaussling.com

Made in the USA
Middletown, DE
24 May 2020